Sidney Crosby

A HOCKEY STORY

PAUL ARSENEAULT

NIMBUS
PUBLISHING

Nimbus Publishing Limited
PO Box 9166
Halifax, NS   B3K 5M8
(902) 455-4286
www.nimbus.ns.ca

Printed and bound in Canada

Design: Troy Cole – Envision Graphic Design

Library and Archives Canada Cataloguing in Publication

   Arseneault, Paul, 1963-
   Sidney Crosby : a hockey story / Paul Arseneault.
   ISBN 1-55109-556-4

1. Crosby, Sidney, 1987– 2. Hockey players—Canada—Biography. I. Title.

GV848.5.C76A78 2005   796.962'092
C2005-906577-X

Canadä̈

The Canada Council | Le Conseil des Arts
for the Arts | du Canada

We acknowledge the financial support of the Government of Canada through the Book Publishing Industry Development Program (BPIDP) and the Canada Council, and of the Province of Nova Scotia through the Department of Tourism, Culture and Heritage for our publishing activities.

Acknowledgements

First, many thanks to Dan Soucoup and Sandra McIntyre at Nimbus Publishing for giving me the opportunity to write this book, and to everyone at Nimbus for their support. Thanks to Heather Bryan at Nimbus for photo research, designer Troy Cole and editor Patricia MacDonald. I would like to thank the coaches, general managers, administrative staff and journalists who added their expertise to this book. I would also like to acknowledge the efforts of research assistant Tom Moore. Thanks also to Mark for his support.

This book is dedicated to the memory of my father, Arthur, and my brother Kenneth.

   —Paul Arseneault

Photo Credits:

Assaff, Peter, 11, 24 bottom

Dahlin, Tom/Hockey Hall of Fame, 1, 17, 18

Dartmouth Heritage Museum, 3

Deschenes, Steve/Hockey Hall of Fame, 54

Dubel Photo Inc., 71 left

Guitard, Flo, 74

Halifax Herald Limited (republished with permission), cover, 7, 9, 13, 20, 21, 41 bottom, 60, 63, 64

Manor, Matthew/Hockey Hall of Fame, 10, 11, 12, 14

McCaughan Photography, 71 right

Nova Scotia Sports Hall of Fame, 4

Pivovarov, Viktor/Moncton Times & Transcript, 22, 24 top, 26, 27, 29, 31, 33, 42, 46, 48, 49, 51

Polk, Matt/Hockey Hall of Fame, b/c, iv, 55, 59

Sandford, Dave/Hockey Hall of Fame, 35, 36, 37, 38, 39, 40, 41 top, 41 middle, 43, 52, 53

Shattuck–St. Mary's School, 15, 19, 20

Table of Contents

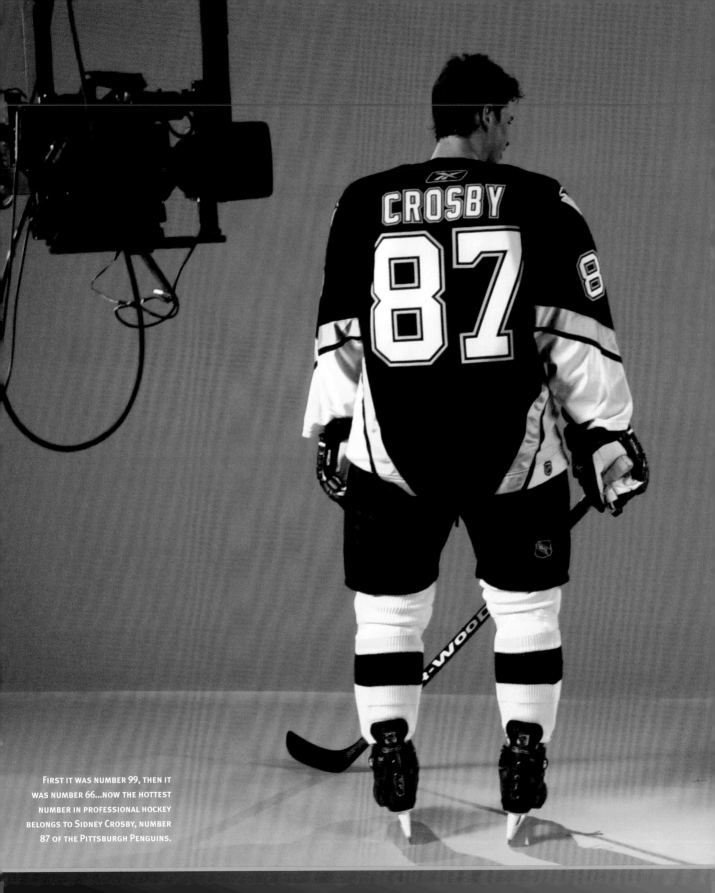

First it was number 99, then it was number 66...now the hottest number in professional hockey belongs to Sidney Crosby, number 87 of the Pittsburgh Penguins.

Foreword

THE FIRST TIME I INTERVIEWED SIDNEY CROSBY, I ASKED HIM TO SHARE WITH ME HIS THREE GOALS IN LIFE. HE REPLIED, "...PLAY HOCKEY FOR A LIVING, PROVIDE FOR MY FAMILY, AND WIN A STANLEY CUP." FIVE YEARS LATER, AT THE TENDER AGE OF EIGHTEEN, HE'S ALREADY ACHIEVED TWO OF THOSE THREE GOALS—AND WHO KNOWS, THE THIRD MAY NOT BE FAR OFF. THAT'S SIDNEY CROSBY. UNSELFISH, MATURE BEYOND HIS YEARS, AND BLESSED WITH LASER BEAM FOCUS. TO PUT IT IN SIMPLE TERMS, HE SETS HIS SIGHTS AND ACHIEVES HIS GOALS.

Away from the game of hockey, I don't pretend to know Crosby very well, but what I have seen, I like. Not only is he a proud Nova Scotian, he's even prouder to be a native of Cole Harbour, Nova Scotia. Whether it's during an appearance on *The Tonight Show with Jay Leno*, before the microphones minutes after being selected number one overall at the NHL entry draft, or during a post game press conference following his Pittsburgh Penguins' debut, geography always comes before celebrity. Where he's from trumps who he is. He's a modest person who comes from humble roots—someone who prefers talking about his family and the people in his neighbourhood to talking about himself. Instead of looking ahead to a career with the Pittsburgh Penguins he has always insisted on reflecting upon his days in minor hockey, acknowledging the former coaches and teammates who, he says, are a big part of his development. I have always believed these characteristics are paramount to what makes him the central figure in a special story to cover, and in many ways they are the primary reasons he is so revered in his home province.

We don't know if Crosby will break Wayne Gretzky's records, or any NHL record for that matter. What we do know is that Sidney Crosby is a young man who brings passion and high purpose to our national game. He has wonderful parents, god-given hockey talent and an outstanding work ethic— all key ingredients that should help lift this young man to the higher echelons of professional hockey.

In arenas across Nova Scotia, like folklore, there are stories about a kid from Cole Harbour who once scored six, seven, even eights points in a game while competing against players three and four years his senior. In junior rinks in Quebec and the Maritimes, fans still whisper about the remarkable teenager who twice led the league in scoring while being named the QMJHL's most valuable player in back-to-back seasons. And now, hockey fans everywhere in the province take what appears to be civic pride when speculating about how successful Crosby will be in the NHL.

In the end, how do you describe the most exciting hockey player ever to come out of Nova Scotia? How does one find the words to describe a young man blessed with not only an abundance of hockey talent, but also a strong character that is essential to his make-up both on and off the ice? Descriptive words are hard to find, although in this book, thanks to some gifted storytelling and thorough research, Paul Arseneault does an excellent job.

—Paul Hollingsworth

Paul Hollingsworth is an anchor/reporter for CTV (Halifax) and a national correspondent for TSN.

Introduction

As the National Hockey League (NHL) regular season gets underway, Canadians are hot with hockey fever as they prepare for a winter *with* pro hockey. Canada's amateur hockey governing body, Hockey Canada, is set to defend Olympic titles in Turin, Italy, in 2006, secure in the knowledge that the program of excellence it launched at the beginning of the millennium has again made Canada the pre-eminent hockey-playing nation in the world. At every level of hockey in Canada, whether it's minor, junior, or adult competitive, registrations are growing, and associations are developing a coordinated vision for the sport from coast to coast. The future of hockey has never looked brighter.

But this is not the same old game. Hockey as we know it is undergoing a profound transition. With the demise of the 2004–2005 NHL season, the glorious generation of Wayne Gretzky and Mario Lemieux came to an abrupt end; with it came the end of a professional hockey era. A labour lockout long in coming forced the NHL and its players to confront issues that had been hurting the league and the sport. Although the short-term pain (a lost 2004–2005 season) was severe, the NHL and the sport of hockey seem to have survived, and the outlook for both is very good.

Convinced that it needed an overhaul to address the lack of creativity and scoring in the game, the NHL, which has always led the way, is enacting a number of rule and style changes that have already begun to filter down through the divisions. But the transformation occurring in the NHL is not just about rules and regulations. There is a definite and marked changing of the guard. A large part of the optimism has to do with the arrival of a talented young player by the name of Sidney Crosby—the new face of the NHL.

Lights, camera, action. Sidney Crosby is a veteran of media relations, having given his first newspaper interview at the age of seven.

FACING PAGE: The rules and the equipment may have changed over the century, but this Dartmouth Hockey League schedule shows that the passion and love for the game remain as strong as ever.

The Rimouski Oceanic graduate and number one draft choice of the Pittsburgh Penguins is a superstar in the making. His stellar minor and junior hockey career has set him up as a future hockey great, in league with Gordie Howe, Gretzky, and Lemieux. Sidney Crosby is not just another young phenom who has arrived to give the sport a temporary boost in popularity; aficionados far and wide concede that he has the "it" factor—that rare combination of intelligence, talent, and grit that sets him above the rest.

Eighteen-year-old Sidney Crosby enters the league with a tremendous arsenal of weapons at his disposal. There has not been a number one draft choice in recent history who can do it all like number 87 can. He can skate, shoot, pass, hit, and lead as well as any of our favourite players. Combine these traits with the fact that he is such a riveting figure—well spoken yet modest—and the National Hockey League now has in its midst a player who can lead the charge as the NHL attempts to rival the National Basketball Association (NBA), the National Football League (NFL), and major league baseball for sports fans' devotion.

Having recently signed a three-year contract worth $850,000 in salary, with generous bonus and incentive riders that will allow him to literally break the bank, the former Dartmouth AAA midget star figures to be a fixture in the NHL for a very long time. With rookie of the year honours and spots on the NHL All-Star Team and Canadian Olympic team up for grabs, Crosby's freshman season promises to be a much-watched and eventful one.

For those who have followed this talented forward's career from his days as a terror in the Metro Halifax Minor Hockey Association to more recent times as the best junior hockey player in Canada with the Rimouski Oceanic, it must seem that Sidney Crosby has been destined for greatness since the moment he laced up a pair of skates. His on-ice wizardry has fans hoping he can re-ignite a sport that has become far too predictable, and his magnetism has convinced many that the game of hockey has found its latest icon.

Nowhere will the fans be more tuned in than in Atlantic Canada, where they cheer one of their own who plays a brand of hockey that Atlantic Canadians have become notorious for. If you talk to teams from the Prairies or central Canada, they will tell you that hockey players from the East Coast are a tough, honest, hard-working lot who neither give nor take a quarter. Although it is true that number 87 has been blessed with the talent to rival any other young hockey player in the world, his grittiness, work ethic, and common touch are what make him a true star in the eyes of Atlantic Canadian hockey fans.

East Coast Roots

Atlantic Canada is the birthplace of hockey. With all due respect to the wonderful folks of Kingston, Ontario, and Montreal, Quebec, the splendid sport has its roots in the province of Nova Scotia.

Dartmouth Hockey League Schedule, 1905.

In addition to Thomas C. Haliburton's now-famous account of the noisy boys of Kings College in Windsor, Nova Scotia, playing "hurley on the long pond on the ice" in the early 1800s, periodicals and books from that era also describe "skaters" brandishing "hurleys" (sticks) and suffering the same sorts of aches and ailments that today's hockey players incur. Missing teeth, broken bones, and injuries to the shins are documented in the news journals of the day. Certainly sounds like the game of hockey, doesn't it?

Of course, every city, town, and hamlet in every province and territory in Canada would love to be able to claim the coolest game on earth as its own, but no one will ever convince Atlantic Canadians that the sport now played in every corner of the world does not have its humble beginnings here. If the depth and degree of passion Atlantic Canadians hold for the game is any indicator, hockey could not have begun anywhere else.

For more than one hundred years, hockey players from the East Coast have been successful in forging noteworthy careers in our national sport. Through the decades, these men and women have taken their talent to the national and international stage—and have left an indelible mark on the game of hockey. From the great Gordie Drillon to the amazing Al MacInnis, from the terrific Thérèse Brisson to the sensational Stacy Wilson, all have done us proud.

Championship hockey teams from the east vying for the right to call themselves Stanley Cup champions were almost commonplace in the early days of Cup competition. Before the National Hockey League claimed Lord Stanley's mug as its own back in 1926, eastern teams regularly held their own championship series play against teams from western and central Canada. Beginning in 1900 and running through the 1912–1913 campaign, no fewer than four Maritime-based hockey clubs battled entries from central Canada for the Stanley Cup.

In the early days of competition, Montreal was home to the best hockey clubs in the land. Following a string of Stanley Cup wins by the Montreal Victorias, the Montreal Shamrocks took over as the city's number one squad. In the 1899–1900 season, on a quest for its second straight cup, the Shamrocks played host to Atlantic Canada's first Stanley Cup challenger, the Halifax Crescents.

Gordie Drillon

Gordie Drillon of Moncton, New Brunswick, was a decorated veteran of the National Hockey League when he retired. A Lady Byng Trophy winner in 1938, Drillon also led the league in scoring that season with 52 points. The consummate team player, the Maple Leaf legend was an all-star in 1938 and 1939 and a Stanley Cup winner in 1942. Although he'll always be remembered as a Toronto Maple Leaf, the Hockey Hall of Fame inductee ended his NHL career as a Hab in 1943.

Al MacInnis

Al MacInnis of Inverness, Nova Scotia, retired in 2005 having played nearly 1,500 games in the National Hockey League. A Norris Trophy winner for best defenceman in 1998–1999, MacInnis also won the Conn Smythe Trophy in 1989 with the Stanley Cup–winning Calgary Flames. A member of the Team Canada squad that captured Olympic gold in Salt Lake City in 2002, the hard-shooting rearguard scored an impressive 1,274 points as a member of the Flames and the St. Louis Blues.

Thérèse Brisson

To many, Thérèse Brisson is the first superstar of women's hockey. The former University of New Brunswick professor played on six world championship squads and was an integral member of Team Canada's gold medal club at the 2002 Olympics. A rock-solid defender who enjoyed the physical part of the game, Brisson joined Team Canada in the mid-1990s and was captain for three years following the 1998 Olympics.

Stacy Wilson

Stacy Wilson of Moncton, New Brunswick, was the very first national women's Olympic hockey team captain. Wilson, a veteran of many national and world championships, led Canada to a silver medal in Nagano, Japan, in 1998. A fiery competitor famous for her work ethic on and off the ice, Wilson moved into the coaching ranks following her retirement, and even had time to write a hockey book for girls in 2000.

These distinguished athletes are the members of the 1898 Halifax Crescents. The capital city club, seen here with the Starr Manufacturing Trophy, was that year's Halifax Hockey League champions.

Led by a very stingy defence, the Crescents were hoping they could avoid a shootout with the heavily favoured Montreal club. It was a game plan that up to that time had put them in good stead. With a forward unit that tended to overwhelm opponents with fast skating and aggressive checking, Halifax had streamrolled opponents throughout the regular and post-season. The Shamrocks, however, were a machine the likes of which Halifax had never encountered.

Despite a valiant effort, the Montreal Shamrocks were just too much for Halifax. The Crescents could not contain the vaunted Montreal offence, and Halifax returned to Nova Scotia victims of 10–2 and 11–0 beatings. The Crescents were no doubt disappointed with the result, but their groundbreaking efforts laid the foundation for other regional clubs confident they could break central Canada's hold on the title.

Buoyed by Halifax's appearance in the Stanley Cup series, two more Nova Scotia–based entries and a New Brunswick side, hungry to bring Atlantic Canada its first Cup victory, also found themselves only one series win away from raising Lord Stanley's Cup aloft.

In 1906, the New Glasgow Cubs, bent on enacting a measure of revenge, tangled with the fabled Montreal Wanderers. Hoping to accomplish what the Halifax Crescents could not, the Cubs headed west. As with the Crescents, though, New Glasgow would meet a Montreal team with just too many weapons. Unable to handle the Wanderers' ferocious attack in game one, New Glasgow fought back gamely and played extremely well in game two. The affair was close throughout, with Montreal eventually pulling out a 7–2 decision on home ice. Finding solace in their second-place finish, the pride of Pictou County returned home with a historic playoff run behind them.

In 1912 and 1913, the Moncton Victorias and the Sydney Miners were the first back-to-back Atlantic Canadian challengers in Stanley Cup history. Both Moncton and Sydney suffered two-game sweeps at the hands of the Quebec Bulldogs, but the defeats were as much about bad timing as bad performances. In most years, either one of these terrific hockey clubs could have won the Stanley Cup outright. Unfortunately, this was the era of the magnificent Joe Malone and the dynamic Quebec Bulldogs, and no team, at that time, was their equal.

In addition to Hall of Famer Joe Malone, Quebec's lineup in 1912–1913 included the stingy Paddy Moran in net as well as famed wingers Tommy Smith and Rusty Crawford. At the height of his career, Malone was a one-man wrecking crew, scoring nine times against Sydney to become one of only a handful of players to score more than eight goals in a Stanley Cup game.

The Bulldogs' reign would last only long enough to deny the Victorias and Miners. Unbelievably, considering how powerful they were, the Quebec

Bulldogs would not successfully challenge for another Cup, yet in consecutive years the short-lived dynasty forced two excellent Maritime entries to settle for second place. The Sydney challenge in 1913 would be the last for a team from the east. In 1926, the National Hockey League took over sole ownership of the trophy, and the dreams of bringing Lord Stanley's mug back to the birthplace of hockey had to be abandoned.

While Atlantic Canadian hockey clubs may have ceased being able to compete for the Stanley Cup after 1926, a steady stream of hockey players continued to play significant and starring roles in professional hockey. On the heels of extraordinary players such as Willie O'Ree, a sort of "golden age" for Atlantic Canada–born hockey players in professional hockey began. From 1965 onward, a plethora of regional elite athletes would rise to the highest ranks of pro hockey: Danny Grant, Keith Brown, Al MacAdam, Gerard Gallant, Gordie Gallant, Bobby Smith, Wendell Young—on and on goes the list of Atlantic Canadians who enjoyed stellar careers in either the National Hockey League or the World Hockey Association.

Success at the professional and international levels has always been the big prize for Atlantic Canadian hockey players, but it would be wrong to think that Atlantic Canada's hockey heritage is all about the professional ranks. The region has also enjoyed incredible success at the amateur and collegiate level.

The Canadian Interuniversity Sport (CIS) championships, emblematic of university hockey superiority, have become a source of pride for a couple of Atlantic schools: The University of Moncton and Acadia University have become collegiate powers in men's hockey, winning six national titles between them.

The Allan Cup, arguably the toughest prize to win in Canadian amateur hockey, has landed in each of the four Atlantic Provinces in the past two decades. Corner Brook, Charlottetown, Saint John, and Truro have each taken turns bringing the senior AAA championship home.

There has also been success in women's hockey. Refusing to be intimidated by much bigger associations coming out of Quebec and Ontario, regional and provincial clubs from the East Coast are taking on the very best competition in the nation and have been distinguishing themselves on a regular basis. One need only look at the results of the Esso Women's Nationals and the fact that Atlantic Canadians continue to contribute big numbers to the national women's program to see how successful women's hockey is in the region.

Hockey for the Future

The successes of the past few decades have helped breed an aura of confidence among young athletes in Atlantic Canada as they strive to reach their dreams of someday playing professional or international hockey. Sidney Crosby is no doubt a product of the great developmental program that has taken root, and his success will in turn spur young hockey players to pursue their athletic goals.

Willie O'Ree

New Brunswick–born hockey player Willie O'Ree forever changed the face of the National Hockey League. The Fredericton native broke the colour barrier in the NHL when the Boston Bruins, unable to deny O'Ree's abundant skills any longer, called him up in January of 1958. O'Ree enjoyed a remarkable career, retiring with the San Diego Hawks of the Pacific Hockey League in 1979. O'Ree continues to help pave the way for players as the director of youth development for the NHL diversity program.

> *"You can't practise what Crosby has. It's just natural. When Sidney Crosby is on the ice, you catch yourself continually watching number 87 because you know at some point the puck will return to him and that he will do something special with it. Off the ice you're so impressed by the way he handles himself ... and more importantly how he handles others."*
>
> — Mario Durocher, former coach of Canada's national junior team

Sidney Crosby's tremendous physical strength is due in large part to his dedicated off-ice workout regimen. During the summer of 2004 he took part in the Los Angeles Kings Development Camp.

FACING PAGE: The summer of 2002 saw Sidney Crosby make one of the most important decisions of his life. The Dartmouth Subways grad is seen sifting through the mound of recruitment packages sent to him. Eventually the fourteen-year-old phenom would settle on Shattuck–St. Mary's prep school in Faribault, Minnesota.

Indeed, Sidney Crosby has become a terrific source of inspiration for hockey players across the region. As noteworthy as his hockey heroics have been, Crosby's class and grace off the ice have been just as impressive, maybe more so. In an era when too many promising young athletes are seen rushing into the stands to confront fans or berating teammates and opponents alike, Sidney Crosby has been a terrific role model for the thousands of Canadian boys and girls who watch him and realize that they too can reach the highest levels of our national sport.

With young stars such as New Glasgow's Colin White, a two-time Stanley Cup winner with New Jersey; P.E.I.'s Brad Richards, who won the Lady Byng Trophy, the Conn Smythe Trophy, and the Stanley Cup in 2004 with Tampa Bay; and Newfoundland's Michael Ryder, an up-and-comer in Montreal, also thriving in the National Hockey League, it certainly appears that Atlantic Canada is about to place itself at the forefront of the professional hockey scene. The region's governing bodies have made an unprecedented commitment to the sport, and it is beginning to pay huge dividends.

Every region of Canada has now sent a young man to the professional ranks to act as its ambassador. In the 1940s and 1950s, a young man from Floral, Saskatchewan, became hockey's first superstar. "Mr. Hockey," as Gordie Howe is known, helped carry the NHL on his shoulders until two young men from Ontario arrived to lighten the load. In the 1970s and 1980s respectively, an extraordinary defenceman from Parry Sound and a scoring sensation from Brantford brought the sport of hockey to prime time. Bobby Orr and Wayne Gretzky combined talents and charisma, helping to raise hockey's profile to the level of football, baseball, and basketball on the North American sports scene.

The last decade saw Quebec's magnificent Mario Lemieux play the game of hockey with a magic that brought patrons of NHL arenas to their feet. Now, it's Atlantic Canada's turn. Nova Scotia's Sidney Crosby is a power forward with unmatchable speed and soft hands. It is a triple threat that no player—with the possible exception of Lemieux—has possessed.

What an exciting time it must be for this particular player—all the opportunities, all the expectations. All things being equal, if fate is kind to Sidney Crosby and allows him to play out his career without falling prey to serious injury or other unfortunate circumstance, the young man from Cole Harbour should have a special NHL career indeed.

1

THE ODYSSEY BEGINS

COLE HARBOUR, NOVA SCOTIA, IS A CHARMING, CLOSE-KNIT COMMUNITY LOCATED IN THE HALIFAX REGIONAL MUNICIPALITY. IN THIS SUBURBAN, MIDDLE-CLASS PART OF DARTMOUTH LIFE REVOLVES AROUND SCHOOL, WORK AND SPORTS, WITH THE POPULAR COLE HARBOUR PLACE AT THE CENTRE. THE COMMUNITY FACILITY, WHICH INCLUDES TWO RINKS, A LIBRARY, SWIMMING POOL, TENNIS AND SQUASH COURTS, THRUMS WITH LIFE. WITH A COMBINED DARTMOUTH–COLE HARBOUR POPULATION OF JUST OVER 80,000, THE REGION IS A BUSY URBAN CENTRE WITH A RURAL PASTORAL FEEL.

While the fixed white cap of the Cole Harbour Lighthouse that looks out over Tor Bay sheds light on a past where mariners ruled the era of wind and water, the local Heritage Farm Museum pays homage to the role that agriculture played in the hamlet founded in the early 1700s. Cole Harbour is most famous for the role it played in the American Revolutionary War of the mid-1700s, acting as a place of refuge for the thousands of Loyalists who left Boston and New York. That claim to fame is about to be overshadowed by an unlikely modern-day hero—a teenage hockey phenom poised to change the landscape of professional hockey.

On August 7, 1987, Sidney Crosby was born in Halifax to Troy and Trina Crosby. Troy Crosby, a native of Halifax himself,

had recently returned home following a major junior hockey career in Verdun that saw him taken in the twelfth round of the 1984 draft by the Montreal Canadiens. It would not take long before his son exhibited a passion for the game as well.

Still a little too young to be streaking down the ice at the local arena, a two-and-a-half-year-old Sidney Crosby retreated to the family basement for his formal introduction to the game of hockey. Using red, white, and blue paint to mimic the contours of a hockey arena, Troy Crosby built his son a hockey hideaway that would allow him the opportunity to hone his skills until it was time to strap on the skates and take his game to the backyard rink.

Quick FACTS

In a sign of things to come, fourteen-year-old Sidney Crosby was featured on the CBC television special *Hockey Day in Canada.*

Sidney Crosby's numbers at Shattuck–St. Mary's were nothing less than spectacular. In a mere fifty-seven games, the first-year phenom scored a remarkable 72 goals and 90 assists for 162 points.

FACING PAGE: Troy, Trina, and Sidney Crosby in June of 2003, soon after hearing that the Shattuck–St. Mary's graduate had been drafted first overall by the Rimouski Oceanic of the QMJHL.

According to Sidney Crosby's own accounts, he was bent on spending every available free moment practising his favourite sport. Long after he had learned to skate, Sidney continued to retreat to the "Crosby Coliseum" to nurture his incredible shooting skills. The countless hours devoted to everything hockey would pay off when the time came for him to join the metro minor hockey scene.

From the moment Sidney Crosby first hit the ice at the tender age of three, it was obvious that the lad could not get enough of the game of hockey. It was also pretty clear that he had been blessed with some incredible talent. Barely old enough to start school, Sidney became something of a local hockey star. Possessing the skills of a player twice his age, the boy was ripping up the metro minor hockey leagues and leaving awe-inspired opponents, teammates, and fans shaking their heads at what they were witnessing.

Regardless of the division, Sidney Crosby was racking up 100-plus-point seasons with regularity and making believers out of teammates and opponents alike. Gary Knickle became a convert when he watched a ten-year-old Sidney tearing up pee wee hockey against his nephew's team: "He's always played with kids three or four years older than him," says Knickle. "It's not so much his hockey, it's his personality and how he carries himself. He shows his maturity" (Canadian Press). At ten years old, Sidney Crosby's hockey profile and stature were growing.

Any time a young hockey phenom starts to put up astronomical numbers and begins to fill arenas the way Sidney Crosby did back in the 1990s, it is only a matter of time before the Canadian media begin to take an interest. In Sidney Crosby's case, he gave his first newspaper interview at the ripe age of seven, although he had been on the radar of national media sources before that. "It was incredible to see the interest in this child athlete," comments Peter Assaff, reporter for the *Northern Light* (Bathurst). "Right away you could see that there was something more to this kid than just goals and assists and the ability to play hockey. Sidney Crosby already had this star quality about him, and Canadians wanted to know as much about him as they could."

By the 2001–2002 hockey season, Sidney Crosby had become a household name—in hockey circles, anyway—from coast to coast. As a fourteen-year-old forward with the Dartmouth Subways, he was about to embark on the most important season of his life. For young hockey players like Crosby who are seriously eyeing the NHL, midget hockey is known as the make it or break it division. To play professional hockey, players need to make their mark at this level, where the pool is bigger and opponents stronger and faster.

While there was never any debate about his skills, nor his ability to put up big numbers, as Sidney Crosby prepared to play his final season in Dartmouth, there were still some observers who questioned whether the fourteen-year-old could match the enormous expectations laid out for him. A national midget tournament in "the City by the Bay" would provide the answers.

UNBEATABLE IN BATHURST: THE 2002 AIR CANADA CUP

ALTHOUGH SIDNEY CROSBY PUT FORTH MANY OUTSTANDING MINOR HOCKEY PERFORMANCES, IT WAS A SINGULAR TOURNAMENT, AND IN PARTICULAR ONE AWE-INSPIRING GAME AGAINST THE RED DEER CHIEFS, THAT SET IN MOTION THE EVENTS THAT WOULD LEAD HIM TO BECOME THIS GENERATION'S HOCKEY ICON. SIDNEY CROSBY USED THE 2002 AIR CANADA CUP, HOSTED BY THE CITY OF BATHURST, NEW BRUNSWICK, TO EXPLODE ONTO THE NORTH AMERICAN HOCKEY SCENE. THE TOURNAMENT MARKED THE BEGINNING OF A JOURNEY THAT WOULD SEE HIM BECOME THE EVENTUAL NUMBER ONE PICK IN THE 2005 NHL ENTRY DRAFT, AND PLACE AN EXCLAMATION MARK ON THE END OF A SPECTACULAR MINOR HOCKEY CAREER IN CANADA.

2002 may well be remembered as the year Sidney Crosby ceased being a local prodigious child talent who amazed patrons of his hometown arena with his athleticism and ability and instead became a bona fide national treasure who was being groomed as professional hockey's heir apparent. The year was noteworthy for Crosby for a number of reasons. There were the numerous on-ice accomplishments and sports milestones he attained one after another, but there were also intriguing off-ice matters that appeared in 2002, specifically a heart-wrenching, life-altering hockey

decision that Crosby and his family would need to make. It is a choice that many other talented young athletes before him have had to make, a virtual rite of passage.

A fifteen-month whirlwind stretch from April 2002 to June 2003 witnessed the transformation of the Cole Harbour, Nova Scotia, minor hockey player from a local to a national to an international hockey name. With amazing speed, Sidney Crosby's hockey and personal life took on new form, and it all began in a northern New Brunswick city that would ultimately share

> **" THE CITY WAS ALREADY VERY EXCITED ABOUT HOSTING THE NATIONAL CHAMPIONSHIPS. BUT WHEN WORD GOT AROUND THAT SIDNEY CROSBY WAS COMING TO TOWN TO PLAY, THE EXCITEMENT AND ANTICIPATION ROSE TO ANOTHER LEVEL. "**
>
> —Peter Assaff, *Northern Light* (Bathurst)

more than one of the young man's defining moments.

In April of 2002, the city of Bathurst was electric in anticipation of playing host to a national hockey championship. The 2002 Air Canada Cup midget championships were to be decided in "the City by the Bay," and the hockey-mad fans of Chaleur were ecstatic.

Since its successful attempt at landing a Quebec Major Junior Hockey League (QMJHL) franchise in 1998 (Acadie-Bathurst Titan), the city had put forth concerted efforts to attract high-profile hockey events for its brand-spanking-new K. C. Irving Regional Centre. Since few national hockey tournaments are bigger or have a higher profile than the storied national midget finals, it seemed that the whole of northern New Brunswick had become enthralled with the bid. The event took on even greater proportions when it became official that the Dartmouth Subway AAA squad and their teenage phenom Sidney Crosby would be in attendance as Team Atlantic's representative.

For some hockey purists, Sidney Crosby's play in this tournament would determine if all the hype surrounding him had been warranted. For years,

Sidney Crosby's acumen in the faceoff circle was developed very early in his career. The Dartmouth Subway centreman is seen taking another crucial draw at the 2002 Air Canada Cup in Bathurst, NB.

One of the questions that dogged Sidney Crosby was going to be addressed in Bathurst as well. Could he still be dominant against players who were taller and bigger? Like the elephant in the room that could no longer be ignored, the question of size and physical strength that had some people unsure of Crosby's future needed to be addressed.

Professional hockey has long been a big man's game. Marcel Dionne and Theoren Fleury aside, dreams of playing pro hockey have become the domain of those six feet tall or taller and two-hundred-plus pounds. Although Sidney Crosby is not a small man by most standards, his physical stature had been a focal point of critics. Convinced his frame could not stand up to the increased punishment it would need to endure the closer he got to the pro ranks, doubters knew the national midget tournament would force-feed Crosby a steady diet of big, fast, talented combatants bent on wearing him down and taking him out of the game. If they succeeded in minimizing the star forward and his impact on games, the critics' concerns would prove justified.

word had been spreading about this young hockey sensation—years ahead of his peers, a once-in-a-lifetime talent who could do amazing things on the ice. This tournament without a doubt would be Sidney Crosby's stiffest challenge to date, and because it was being held on a national stage, its significance would be magnified. Of course, this would not be the first time Sidney Crosby was tested against rival national competition, but undeniably it would be one of the most important.

Sidney Crosby needed to go to Bathurst and perform well, put up some impressive numbers, and show that he could play through being the marked man. Every team playing against Dartmouth was going to key on Crosby, and he needed to show that he could produce despite the constant attention he'd receive from opposing checkers. Indeed, Crosby would be expected to stand out among the midget-aged elite, most of whom were feeling the pressure of trying to impress major junior or college scouts themselves.

Sidney Crosby celebrates another Team Atlantic score. The fourteen-year-old did a lot of celebrating at the national midget championship, taking home both the top scorer and most valuable player awards at the event.

ABOVE: Though few observers gave Team Atlantic much of a chance at winning gold at the 2002 Air Canada Cup, Sidney Crosby and his mates nearly pulled it off, going the distance before losing 6–2 to Tisdale, Saskatchewan, in the final.

Northern New Brunswick played a big role in Sidney Crosby's hockey life in 2002 and 2003. After leading his Dartmouth AAA Subways to the Air Canada Cup in Bathurst in April of 2002, Crosby returned to the region the following winter as a member of Team Nova Scotia during the Canada Winter Games held in Campbellton-Bathurst.

Facing Page: Sidney Crosby's final season as a member of the Darmouth AAA Subways saw him put up some spectacular numbers, including a franchise record 106 goals scored in 81 games.

the Canadian Hockey League (CHL) ranks, or it would see him fail and take a significant step backwards in what to that point had been a meteoric and unblemished rise.

Hockey fans in Bathurst had waited a long time for this calibre of hockey to come to their city. The patience the fans and organizers had shown was rewarded with some truly spectacular play. Unlike in years past, the national midget-aged talent pool was extremely deep in 2002, and each and every regional rep at this event belonged. Parity at long last appeared to have arrived in Canadian amateur hockey, and the state of the game was healthier than ever.

In the days leading up to the official opening, fans were salivating at the prospect of seeing Sidney Crosby lead Team Atlantic against the best midget-aged talent in the nation; one game in particular, though, stands head and shoulders above them all. On Wednesday, April 24, the Pacific representatives, the Red Deer Chiefs, would take on Team Atlantic rep Dartmouth, and followers of the event knew that this match had all the earmarks of a classic.

The Red Deer Chiefs played a typical western Canadian style of hockey. The Chiefs were big, rugged, and fast, and they finished their checks with a ferocity that intimidated most opponents. In their key round-robin match against Team Atlantic, their game plan was obvious to all: Place a bull's eye on Sidney Crosby's jersey, and hit him at every opportunity. Every time Crosby touched the puck, and maybe a few times when he didn't, he was to be punished.

As unfair as it may seem, on the eve of the championships, Sidney Crosby's young career was already at a crossroads. This was a week that was either going to see him take his game to another level and set the stage for his eventual leap to

Even for a guy as tough as Sidney Crosby, who is not known for shying away from the rough stuff, the task of playing through the chaos and getting on the scoreboard must have seemed a daunting one. "Everyone in the building, including probably Sidney Crosby, knew what Red Deer's game plan was going to be," notes Crosby's Dartmouth Subways coach Brad Crossley. "Nail Crosby at every turn, and make him a non-issue in the game."

The game plan may have been sound, but someone obviously forgot to tell Sidney Crosby. He was unstoppable, despite the Chiefs' best efforts to hit him at every turn. Against the feared Red Deer machine from Alberta, Crosby scored a natural hat trick and added two assists as the Subways surged to a 5–0 first period lead.

The western reps must have wondered what had hit them as shift after shift Crosby disposed of opposing checkers and double teams to find the

back of the net. Crosby would not be denied. It was an awesome sight to watch him defy Red Deer to use physical force to stop him and then dispose of the tight checking on his way to potting another goal. It was a period of hockey for the ages and one still talked about by those in attendance. "Sidney Crosby was determined to send a message not only to the Red Deer Chiefs, but to anyone who doubted his ability to be a star on the national stage," adds coach Crossley.

Ultimately, Dartmouth's substantial first period lead evaporated as Red Deer's vaunted offensive arsenal kicked in. The Alberta squad eventually found their game, and the underdog Dartmouth Subways were subdued 8–6. The final outcome that afternoon quickly became an afterthought, an irrelevant asterisk linked to one of the truly superior solo efforts in event lore. Sidney Crosby had proved that when confronted with the best midget-aged hockey opposition in the nation, he was still head and shoulders above them. He was the best of the best in his age group, and the gap between him and everyone else seemed to be growing.

Of course, the round-robin match would not be the last the Red Deer Chiefs would see of

Quick FACTS

In November of 2003, Sidney Crosby made headlines across North America with the infamous "lacrosse goal" he scored against the Quebec Remparts.

While with the Rimouski Oceanic, Sidney Crosby became the first player to win the prestigious CHL Player of the Year award in consecutive seasons (2003–2004, 2004–2005).

Sidney Crosby won the Guy Lafleur Trophy (most valuable player in the QMJHL playoffs) on the strength of a spectacular post-season total of 31 points in 13 games.

Quick FACTS

In a round-robin match at the 2002 Air Canada Cup in Bathurst, New Brunswick, Sidney Crosby scored five unanswered points in the first period against the powerhouse Red Deer Chiefs. Crosby's three-goal, two-assist opening-frame effort vaulted him onto the national hockey stage.

ABOVE: Sidney Crosby prepares to take to the ice at the K. C. Irving Regional Centre. The city of Bathurst was electric with the news that Sidney Crosby would be coming to town to participate in the 2002 Air Canada Cup.

FACING PAGE: Sidney Crosby enjoying a brief respite from the rink. J. P. Parisé, Shattuck–St. Mary's director of hockey operations, marvelled at the way the young superstar handled all of the attention with quiet grace and a maturity well beyond his years.

Sidney Crosby. Determined to savour the sweet taste of revenge, Crosby and his mates would turn the tables on the Chiefs on semifinal Saturday. Displaying a flare for dramatics that had become as much a part of his game as goals and assists, Sidney Crosby scored a power play marker with thirty-two seconds remaining in the game to give his team a 4–3 come-from-behind victory. The last-minute heroics propelled Dartmouth into the finals and sent rival Red Deer to the proverbial showers.

To Crosby's most ardent fans and harshest critics, the tournament proved to be a revelation. To those not previously sold on his game, Crosby emphatically answered all remaining questions. And to those who believed in the young man's talent, even they must have been surprised at just how good he was. In the end, his sensational play in Bathurst underscored something more than the obvious fact that Sidney Crosby was indeed the best minor hockey player in Canada. Having faced

down every hurdle that had come his way during his years in Nova Scotia, it was clear that Sidney Crosby faced the biggest decision in his life—whether or not to leave home to pursue his hockey dreams.

AIR CANADA CUP TOURNAMENT STATISTICS, BATHURST, N.B., APRIL 2002

	GP	G	A	P	PIM	GWG
Sidney Crosby	5	8	10	18	6	2

3

YOUNG MAN GOES WEST

SIDNEY CROSBY'S DOMINATING PERFORMANCE AT THE 2002 AIR CANADA CUP IN BATHURST UNDERLINED THE NEED FOR THE TALENTED YOUNG MAN TO SEEK OUT NEW CHALLENGES. HAVING ACCOMPLISHED EVERYTHING HE COULD IN ATLANTIC CANADA, HE WAS FACED WITH THE PROSPECT OF LEAVING HOME TO PURSUE HIS HOCKEY GOALS.

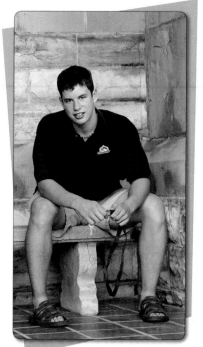

The spring of 2002 saw Sidney Crosby quickly approaching a crossroads … and the path he chose would decide his future in the game. For most small-town Canadians who dream of playing in the NHL, there comes a moment when they must face the heart-wrenching reality that advancing their careers will mean leaving home. It had probably been a moment that Sidney Crosby knew would arrive; still, for a boy of fourteen, one can only imagine how agonizing it was to think of leaving home so young.

In his autobiography, *The Great One*, Wayne Gretzky admits that one of the most difficult decisions he had to make in his life was to leave home at the age of fourteen. With few if any hockey challenges remaining in his hometown of Brantford, Ontario, a teenage Gretzky grudgingly acknowledged the need to leave the safety and security of his boyhood home for the opportunity to play in the famed Toronto minor hockey system.

Certainly Sidney Crosby had some of the same misgivings in the summer of 2002. But the need to leave his Nova Scotia home, as painful as it must have been, would have been clear. The kind of competition that Crosby needed in order to adequately prepare for a role in major junior hockey could only be found elsewhere. In time, the question evolved from whether or not to leave to where his new hockey home would be. For the potential number one pick in the 2003 junior entry draft, it was a decision not to be taken lightly.

Quick FACTS

In 2002–2003, Sidney Crosby packed up his hockey bag and headed west, where he attended Shattuck–St. Mary's prep school in Faribault, Minnesota, helping the Sabres to a U.S. national midget championship.

In 1967, the National Hockey League held a monumental expansion. Six new hockey clubs—the St. Louis Blues, Minnesota North Stars, Philadelphia Flyers, Los Angeles Kings, California Seals, and Pittsburgh Penguins—joined the "original six" clubs in the new-look NHL.

In many respects, Sidney Crosby's 2002–2003 season would act as a bridge. He needed to get from where he was, a minor hockey superstar with unlimited potential, to where he was going, the number one, most sought after junior hockey player in the Canadian Hockey League.

Sidney Crosby's camp understood that he needed to be challenged, he needed to be groomed, he needed to be surrounded by hockey people who understood what this year was about. The Cole Harbour native needed to go to an organization that would allow him the opportunity to develop not only as a hockey player but also as a person. It also needed to provide Sidney Crosby the opportunity to attain a national hockey championship.

Any number of teams would have deemed it an out-and-out coup to land a player of Crosby's stature, but eventually the impressive list of potential hockey homes got whittled down to one midwestern prep school. It was a selection that was as intriguing to some as it was surprising.

Shattuck–St. Mary's prep school is located in Faribault, Minnesota. The school had enjoyed a history of success prior to 2002–2003, and Sidney Crosby was brought on board to help the Sabres win another national championship.

Despite its storied hockey history, the small and somewhat unremarkable midwestern institution appeared to some to be an odd choice as the new home for the budding hockey superstar. A closer look and it becomes clear why this prairie powerhouse was actually perfect.

To begin with, the relatively low profile of Shattuck–St. Mary's added to its attractiveness. The onslaught of media and other distractions, at least early on, was not as great here as it would have been had Crosby remained in Canada or attended an East Coast institution. The young man would certainly benefit from the early anonymity while he adjusted to his new surroundings.

In addition, one of the prerequisites in choosing a school was the ability to surround Crosby with established hockey people. At Shattuck–St. Mary's, the hockey program director had direct ties to one of Canada's most glorious hockey moments. In 1972, J. P. Parisé was a member of Team Canada during the unforgettable Summit Series against the USSR. The Minnesota North Stars winger had become infamous for his role in a game-eight uprising against West German referee Kompalla, which ended with Parisé's ejection from the deciding match.

Thirty years later, Parisé had completed the impressive transition from NHL star to prep-school administrator, and he would be seen as the perfect mentor for Sidney Crosby. With Parisé's son Zach, a graduate of the Sabres program, also on the cusp of accelerating his own pro hockey aspirations, it must have seemed like an ideal situation.

More and more it appeared that the decision to go to Faribault was the right one, and after some initial trepidation and concerns about the unfamiliar surroundings both on and off the ice, Sidney Crosby began to show everyone why he was pegged as the best midget-aged hockey prospect in North America.

With fellow standouts Jack Johnson and Drew Stafford riding shotgun, Sidney Crosby helped the Sabres get out of the gate quickly—and they did not look back. In approximately seventy games, Shattuck–St. Mary's sported a win-loss record of well over .500. The club travelled extensively in the United States and Canada and racked up impressive victory after impressive victory, including two over long-time Canadian arch-rivals the Calgary Royals and the Edmonton Canadians.

With Sidney Crosby firing on all cylinders, the Sabres finished the 2002–2003 season playing perhaps their best hockey of the year. As the regular season drew to a close, there was absolutely no doubt that Crosby's outstanding performance had locked up his status as the number one pick at the upcoming QMJHL June draft. With his standing as the number one junior prospect in the world assured, Sidney Crosby took aim at the national championship.

As the playoffs began, the familiar story of opponents centring their entire game plan on shutting down Sidney Crosby came to the fore. The U.S. national midget championship would be settled in the nation's capital, and Sidney Crosby was aware that a number of familiar opponents would descend on the District of Columbia bent on denying him the title.

Sabres bench boss Tom Ward knew his club was in tough, but there was something about Sidney Crosby's demeanour that had a calming influence on both the coach and his club: "You could sense that Sidney felt very confident about his game and also very secure in how well the team had been playing prior to the national championship."

A veteran of these national midget championships himself, coach Ward also noticed a heightened degree of determination and focus by the rookie. "I could sense heading into the playoffs that Sidney was not going to be denied. It was exciting to see how Sidney had

The most impressive weapon in Sidney Crosby's arsenal may be his tremendous shot.

prepared himself for the moment. He was an important cog in a talented and veteran team that as a collective group recognized the importance of another national championship to the Shattuck–St. Mary's hockey program." Ward's keen intuition was dead on: Sidney Crosby would end up playing some of the best hockey of his life in the 2003 post-season.

The Little Caesars team from Detroit, Michigan, and the Midget Tier 1 Stars from Dallas, Texas, were the next to confront Sidney Crosby and his Shattuck–St. Mary's side. The Little Caesars squad had played well against the Sabres in the past, earning a reputation for tough, aggressive play. The Dallas Stars, on the other hand, were known for balance and depth and their consistency of play. Knowing full well that all roads to the national championship went through Sidney Crosby, both clubs took aim at the Sabres' leading scorer. If their intent was to intimidate Crosby and put him off his game, their plan backfired in a huge way.

Confronting perhaps the most sustained physical opposition in quite some time, Crosby both dished out and absorbed a lot of punishment. The physical play seemed to inspire him even more as he helped engineer wins over both Detroit and Dallas. There is no doubt that opponents enjoyed some success in slowing down the Shattuck–St. Mary's star, but as the Senators, Little Caesars, and Stars all found out, Sidney Crosby was becoming adept at making the on-ice adjustments needed to deal with the strategies opposing coaches were throwing at him.

ABOVE: Sidney Crosby and the rest of the Shattuck–St. Mary's starting unit prepare for a match during the 2002–2003 season. Crosby, along with top-flight prospects Jack Johnson and Drew Stafford, would lead the Minnesota prep school to a national midget hockey championship.

FACING PAGE: Sidney Crosby tries to get away from his check during a regular season game at Shattuck–St. Mary's.

The Shattuck–St. Mary's Sabres would need to dispose of some familiar foes to once again reign as national champions … and Sidney Crosby would need to be the X factor against some very tough competition. The Eastern Massachusetts Senators were a skilled team that featured as many offensive weapons as the Sabres. All things being equal, the Senators may have been the Sabres' biggest competition and an awesome early threat, but Sidney Crosby would prove to be too much for the team from New England. The Sabres escaped with a victory and the right to move on.

The final obstacle to the national championship came in the form of the very skilled and very hungry Team Illinois, whose big guns included five-foot, ten-inch sniper Kyle Acre, as well as the strong goaltending tandem of Johnny Riley and Mike Devoney.

> *"SIDNEY CROSBY ALWAYS HANDLED HIMSELF EXTREMELY WELL. WITH ALL OF THE DISTRACTIONS AND DISRUPTION THAT HE HAS HAD TO ENDURE THIS YEAR, FOR HIM TO BE ABLE TO COMPORT HIMSELF THE WAY HE HAS AND TO HAVE THE KIND OF SEASON HE IS HAVING ON THE ICE, I THINK IT SAYS A LOT ABOUT HIS CHARACTER AND HIS DESIRE.*
> —J. P. Parisé, director of hockey operations, Shattuck–St. Mary's

Sidney Crosby and the other Sabres forwards would face their stiffest challenge to date. Illinois boasted a solid defensive corps and an opportunistic forward attack that specialized in capitalizing on goal-scoring chances. The midwestern hockey team was also a confident bunch, having posted a gold medal victory earlier in the season at the prestigious Mac Midget Hockey Tournament in Calgary, Alberta.

As expected, the final was an out-and-out war. Like a Frazier–Ali fight, both teams threw their best punches without garnering a knock-down. With ten minutes left in the game, Shattuck–St. Mary's was up by two and thwarting every offensive thrust put forth by the Illinois club. As time became a factor, it looked as though Team Illinois had run out of answers for the stifling Sabres trap, as had been the case throughout the 2002–2003 season.

However, the Illinois players were also at their most dangerous when their backs were up against the wall. With less than a minute left in the game, Team Illinois pulled their goaltender. After a frantic scramble in front of the Sabres net, J. J. Evans tucked the puck behind the surprised Shattuck–St. Mary's keeper, and Team Illinois had pulled within one. Team Illinois had recaptured the momentum and looked as if they were primed to tie the affair, but the boys from Minnesota had not come this far to be denied the gold, and the Sabres would hang on for the 5–4 victory.

The national championship capped a sensational season for Sidney Crosby. In fifty-seven games played, he accumulated 72 goals and 90 assists for 162 points. The points-per-game average of almost 3 was absolutely off the chart—and it still did not do justice to the strength of his play, game in and game out.

Perhaps the most important accomplishment in 2002–2003 for Sidney Crosby was the title victory. He had proved that he could take a team on his shoulders and make it a winner. The centreman had succeeded in making every Sabres player around him better, a talent shared by all great ones. With all his pre-season aspirations seemingly met, Sidney Crosby would be able to return to Canada from his one-

Quick FACTS

Sidney Crosby was all of sixteen years, four months, and twenty-four days old when he established a World Junior Championship record by becoming the youngest player to score a goal. Crosby achieved the historic feat on December 28, 2003, during a 7–2 Team Canada win over Switzerland.

year hiatus and take a well-deserved break from the frenetic pace.

While Shattuck–St. Mary's may have provided Sidney Crosby some early respite, as his accomplishments and profile began to skyrocket, so did the demands of fans, the media, and a public hungry to know more about him. It must have been difficult trying to juggle all of these requests while still trying to devote his energies to making his hockey club a winner.

Through it all, though, Crosby remained approachable, humble, and personable. The Shattuck–St. Mary's experience was not just about the growth of his game; it was also about his evolution as a person. As happy as those close to him were with his on-ice advancement, Sidney Crosby's obvious development as a confident, mature, articulate young man must have made friends and family proud. Even more impressive was that he was able to foster this evolution as the demands on his time and his energies increased markedly.

You can be certain that the Rimouski Oceanic of the QMJHL had also been taking stock of Crosby's ability both to stay cool and to lead a franchise to the winner's circle. With only months left before the 2003 QMJHL entry draft, Rimouski ownership must have felt as if they were holding the winning lottery ticket.

Even on vacation Sidney Crosby was never very far from the game of hockey. Back home from Minnesota for a few days, he decided to take in some international hockey action at the Metro Centre as Slovakia and the Czech Republic met up for an exhibition game.

FACING PAGE:
Number 87 gets ready to lead his charges onto enemy ice at the Halifax Metro Centre.

SIDNEY FRANCHISE: THE ARRIVAL OF NUMBER 87 TO THE Q

JUNE IS THE MONTH OF RENEWAL IN THE HOCKEY UNIVERSE. OPTIMISM REIGNS SUPREME AS TEAMS PREPARE TO RESTOCK THEIR CLUBS WITH FRESH BLOOD THROUGH THEIR SELECTIONS IN THE ANNUAL ENTRY DRAFT. WHETHER IT BE THE NHL OR THE CHL, THE DRAFT IS AN OPPORTUNITY TO REPLENISH AND REBUILD, AN INVITATION TO WIPE THE SLATE CLEAN AND BEGIN THE PROCESS OF BUILDING A WINNING TEAM OR REMAINING ONE. ALTHOUGH EVERY YEAR'S DRAFT IS GREETED WITH KEEN ANTICIPATION, THE 2003 QUEBEC MAJOR JUNIOR HOCKEY LEAGUE DRAFT TOOK ON ADDED SIGNIFICANCE. THE 2003 FIRST-OVERALL SELECTION WOULD NOT BE SOME TALENTED PLAYER WHO HAD A BETTER-THAN-EVEN SHOT OF MAKING THE ROSTER AND STICKING AROUND FOR THE SEASON; THIS TOP PICK WAS THE MOST TALKED ABOUT TEENAGER SINCE ERIC LINDROS.

Sidney Crosby would make his franchise the hottest ticket in the league, and his league the most talked about circuit in the sport. For most, there would be no suspense in terms of where he would begin his QMJHL career. The Rimouski Oceanic owned the first pick in 2003, and that is where Crosby would play. But as the days and weeks flew by, it occurred to some that maybe something other than the obvious would happen. For those who remembered the draft of 2001, Sidney Crosby's selection by Rimouski was not yet a sure thing!

In June of 2001, the QMJHL was prepared to hold one of the deepest drafts in the league's history. Although it had been assumed for months that the first selection would be Steve Bernier, a scoring machine out of Ste.-Foy, Quebec, a draft-day blockbuster seemed imminent to some observers.

Considering that future Sidney Crosby linemates Marc-Antoine Pouliot and Dany Roussin, along with highly touted NHL prospects Stephen Dixon of Halifax and Danny

Sidney Crosby stops on a dime to elude a Moncton Wildcat defender. Crosby's lower-body strength affords him amazing balance on the blades.

Stewart of Charlottetown, were also available in the draft, it would not have been a complete surprise to see a major deal unfold. Ultimately the Moncton Wildcats, sold on the incredible upside that a Steve Bernier choice offered, settled on the future first-round selection of the San Jose Sharks.

The 2001 experience certainly provided food for thought in 2003. Would Rimouski dare trade away Sidney Crosby in order to secure future first-round draft picks? Would they entertain a four- or five-player package deal that would give them instant depth and a secure shot at making the QMJHL playoffs for a number of years?

On Saturday, June 7, 2003, le Palais des sports in Val-d'Or, Quebec, was filled to capacity as QMJHL president Gilles Courteau began proceedings. Sidney Crosby's eagerly anticipated arrival into the ranks of major junior hockey was about to become reality. On cue, a gentleman settled in easily behind his microphone to make an announcement. Was a trade in the offing, or was Sidney Crosby about to become the newest member of the Rimouski Oceanic?

The Raising of the Oceanic

With a single entry-draft selection of a sixteen-year-old centreman, the Rimouski Oceanic set in motion the redefinition of a franchise and the resurgence of a league. For the Oceanic, the arrival of the peerless Shattuck–St. Mary's grad in June of 2003 meant a hastened escape from the abyss and a return to national junior hockey prominence. For the QMJHL, Sidney Crosby's appearance in the double blue of Rimouski signalled a welcome surge of national and international attention, the likes of which it had never enjoyed before, and changed the dynamic of the circuit in every respect, from league attendance to franchise expansion.

The Rimouski Oceanic's quest for national junior hockey supremacy began in 1995. Having revived the defunct St.-Jean Lynx operation, team management methodically transformed itself into a legitimate contender by the beginning of the new millennium. The Oceanic, led by Prince Edward Island standouts Brad Richards and Thatcher Bell, played an up-tempo style that tended to overwhelm opposing defensive schemes. By the beginning of the 1999–2000 season, Rimouski had its sights squarely set on the city of Halifax and that year's Memorial Cup tournament.

The Oceanic were clearly the class of the QMJHL that season. A record of forty-eight wins and twenty losses along with four ties gave notice that they would be the prohibitive favourites to win the President's Cup, the trophy emblematic of Quebec Major Junior Hockey League superiority. A tough final-series win provided the perfect dress rehearsal for a Memorial Cup that saw the Oceanic go through the week-long tournament undefeated. In the final against Barrie of the Ontario Hockey League (OHL), Rimouski easily manhandled the Colts and strode to a 6–2 title-game victory.

In less than a decade of operation, the Rimouski Oceanic, through a combination of shrewd draft picks and sound management, had risen to the top of the junior hockey heap. Rimouski's rise to the national junior hockey summit was thoroughly impressive, but success would come at a hefty price, and the team would soon find itself struggling to escape the second division.

In the years following the win in Halifax, Rimouski's fortunes took a nosedive. Heavily dependent on senior players during their suc-

Quick FACTS

Sidney Crosby led Rimouski, which had missed the 2003 playoffs, back to the post-season in 2004. Following a quarterfinal win over Shawinigan, the Moncton Wildcats ended Sidney Crosby's rookie playoff run.

Sidney Crosby will be one very rich teenager. Reebok, the giant U.S. manufacturer, signed the eighteen-year-old professional hockey player to a lucrative multi-year deal.

An all-around athletic talent, Sidney Crosby won an Atlantic Canadian baseball championship with the Cole Harbour Cardinals in 1998.

Sidney Crosby shakes off a check and awaits a feed from a linemate.

The Dynamic Duo. Marc-Antoine Pouliot and Sidney Crosby were probably the most explosive tandem in the QMJHL in 2004–2005.

cessful Memorial Cup run, the eventual graduation and departure of experienced leaders such as Richards (to the Tampa Bay Lightning), Juraj Kolnik (to the N.Y. Islanders), and goalie Sébastien Caron (to the Pittsburgh Penguins) left a chasm in the Rimouski lineup that raw rookie draft picks could not fill. Just three years after their national championship win, the Oceanic sat last in the QMJHL standings.

In 2002–2003, the Rimouski Oceanic managed a paltry 25 points in seventy-two games. The team's eleven wins were the worst in team history, and their sixteenth-place finish in the association was one worse than their previous low. For the first time in their existence, they were forced to watch the post-season festivities from the sidelines.

Despite their humbling bout with adversity, Rimouski garnered little sympathy from CHL rivals. Ironically, it would have been easy to understand if teams had actually been envious of Rimouski's fall. While some CHL organizations struggle in obscurity and mediocrity for decades, just three years removed from a national championship, the Oceanic were about to welcome an all-world talent to their roster. Rimouski was about to become the sole ben-

eficiary of a once-in-a-lifetime talent. Those experts who predicted that Crosby's impact would be immediate and immeasurable could not have been more correct.

From the moment Crosby arrived at camp in August of 2003, the fortunes of the Rimouski Oceanic hockey club rose. The fan base in the hockey-mad town had been thoroughly reignited once again, and the on-ice product had been given instant credibility. The great hockey fans in Rimouski, it seemed, had welcomed number 87 with open arms.

The relationship between Crosby and his mates also seemed to be very good. Teammates admired him and his abilities, while coaches lauded his team-first attitude. Eric Neilson recalls the impression Crosby made: "The first game I ever saw him play, me and [teammate] Mark Tobin were in the stands watching him get point after point. Toby looked over at me and said, 'Darryl Sittler [Leafs Hall of Famer] right there'" (The Crosby Connection).

While it is obvious that Sidney Crosby understood that the expectations in Rimouski were sky-high,

a comment he made following his selection by the Nics put everything into perspective: "Scoring goals and making plays is part of my job. I didn't come with any expectations prior to the season. I'm playing hockey, I'm having fun, and I enjoy it" (The Crosby Connection).

Sidney Crosby's rookie season of 2003–2004 was smashing. It seemed that every game featured an exciting third period come-from-behind win, or another record-breaking performance before another sellout crowd. The storybook season kept getting bigger and better, reaching its crescendo with a dramatic midwinter spectacle in the province's capital.

On a brisk February night in 2004, Sidney Crosby and the Rimouski Oceanic rolled into town to take on the beloved Remparts. With great expectations, 15,333 rabid Remparts fans packed le Colisée to see their team welcome their provincial rivals. It was the kind of attendance figure normally reserved for NHL arenas, and it was an unmistakable sign that Sidney Crosby had a special aura about him. Like Gretzky or Lemieux, Crosby drew capacity crowds regardless of the standings, regardless of the schedule. He alone was worth the price of admission, and that put him in very select company indeed.

Riding the coattails of Sidney Crosby's smashing 54-goal, 81-assist freshman season, the Oceanic climbed ten spots in league standings, finishing with 76 points and adding well over twenty games to the win column. In addition, they enjoyed a return to playoff action, emerging victorious from a quarterfinal-round battle with Shawinigan, only to be subdued eventually by the Moncton Wildcats. As great as the 2003–2004 season was, Sidney Crosby and the Rimouski Oceanic would be even better the next year.

In the 2004–2005 season, the Oceanic secured forty-five wins, including an amazing second-half record that assured the club its best regular season ever. Sidney Crosby, assisted by his talented linemates Dany Roussin and Marc-Antoine Pouliot, played like a man on a mission. "Sidney was just incredible in these playoffs," says Acadie-Bathurst coach Mario Durocher. "The kid was just unstoppable."

Despite Crosby's appearance in the World Junior Championship, which forced him to miss some league games, the dynamic power forward put up brilliant numbers: 66 goals and 102 assists for 168 points placed him first in league scoring and secured his credentials as the CHL's top player for the second year in a row.

As good as the regular season was for both the fans and for Sidney Crosby, the 2005 QMJHL playoff run was even more spectacular and proved once again that in pressure situations, Sidney Crosby seemed to be able to dig down and find another level to

Quick FACTS

In a Memorial Cup semifinal game that will be talked about for some time, number 87 scored three goals and two assists to lead his Rimouski Oceanic team to a 7–4 decision over the Ottawa 67's.

Sidney Crosby reportedly rejected an offer of $7.5 million over three years to sign with Hamilton of the World Hockey Association.

Out of the Kelowna Rockets, the London Knights, the Ottawa 67's, and the Calgary Hitmen, the only CHL club that did not face Sidney Crosby in the 2005 Memorial Cup is the Calgary Hitmen.

Classic Crosby. One of Sidney Crosby's greatest traits as a player is his attention to detail. Here he drives to the net with his stick on the ice and his eyes locked on the puck.

nents, each with their own set of intangibles that the Oceanic needed to address. In fact, Rimouski's first opponent, the Lewiston MAINEiacs, buoyed by an impressive first-round upset over the favoured Shawinigan Cataractes, felt their club might just be primed to derail the mighty Oceanic train before it ever really got rolling.

The Lewiston MAINEiacs had finished the 2004–2005 campaign in fourth place in the Eastern Division, some 26 points behind Rimouski. At first glance the series looked very one sided. The season series saw the Oceanic take three games of four against the U.S.-based club, with many of those not as close as the scores indicated. Still, there were some X factors that seemed to give the MAINEiacs more than a fighting chance against Rimouski. To begin with, Lewiston enjoyed momentum coming off the series with the Cataractes, while Rimouski had gone more than a week without game-day competition. In addition, Lewiston was led by a talented duo capable of engineering an upset of this magnitude. Columbus Blue Jackets draft pick Alexandre Picard and New York Rangers blue-line prospect Jonathan Paiement gave the MAINEiacs a solid one-two punch that Rimouski needed to counter.

his play. Game after game, round after round, he got stronger, more dominant, and more determined. With his leadership skills at the forefront, Crosby consistently willed his teammates to better playoff performances. In order, Lewiston, Chicoutimi, and Halifax fell by the wayside as Crosby and company, with surgical precision, cut through opposition defences and shifted their high-powered offence into overdrive.

The Oceanic's stunning playoff stats do not tell the whole story, though. Each series saw Rimouski have to battle tooth and nail to subdue oppo-

In addition to having some bona fide talent on their roster, Lewiston enjoyed the luxury of no expectations. While Rimouski was expected to win easily over its American counterpart, the MAINEiacs were not expected to go far. Rimouski coach Doris Labonte feared as much, no doubt aware that Lewiston could play with reckless abandon. The MAINEiacs had little to lose as the 2005 QMJHL playoffs began, and that made them very dangerous.

Any suggestion that Lewiston might be intimidated by beginning the series in the raucous Colisée de Rimouski was summarily dismissed by the third period. Benefiting from a needless Rimouski penalty, Lewiston's Alexandre Picard continued his dynamite playoff effort by blasting a shot past Rimouski keeper Cédrick Desjardins. The marker gave the 2005 QMJHL's Cinderella story a 3–2 lead with less than twenty minutes to play.

It seemed that the Rimouski Oceanic were already facing the defining moment in their 2005 playoff run. A Lewiston opening-game victory might just give the underdog the confidence it needed to pull the upset off. In the minutes that followed Picard's go-ahead marker, the Oceanic would have to answer one question: Were they a contender or a pretender? It didn't take long for Crosby and company to decide it was time for the clock to strike midnight on Cinderella.

Beginning with a crucial counter by Danny Stewart, the Oceanic scored four consecutive third period goals on their opponents. Lewiston goalie Jaroslav Halak could not shut down Rimouski's high-powered scoring machine. The Oceanic had dodged a bullet as the top seed rebounded to take the game 6–3.

The eruption of offence in the final frame of game one appeared to change the whole complexion of the series. Opening-game jitters were replaced by confidence and self-assuredness in

games two, three, and four. The Oceanic's strut had reappeared, and that spelled doom for coach Clément Jodoin and his Lewiston club.

In the previous three games, a combination of outstanding goaltending by Edmundston, New Brunswick, native Cédrick Desjardins and back-to-back-to-back monster performances by

Sidney Crosby accepts congratulations from teammates after scoring a crucial third-period marker against the Wildcats.

A New Era for the QMJHL

While Sidney Crosby's arrival ignited the resurgence of a former champion to its rightful place among the CHL's elite teams, it also signalled the beginning of a new era for the Quebec Major Junior Hockey League. Arguably, the least recognized of the three CHL entities before Crosby's selection in the June draft of 2003, the QMJHL stepped out of the shadows afterwards and overtook the Ontario Hockey League (OHL) and Western Hockey League (WHL) as the most important junior hockey league in the nation.

Sidney Crosby's role in the revitalization was key. Perhaps no junior hockey player before him has had such a positive influence on his respective league. Since number 87's arrival in "the Q," his influence in the areas of league attendance, increased national and international exposure, and perhaps most importantly expansion cannot be overstated.

One glance at the attendance figures the year before Sidney Crosby arrived (2002–2003) compared with those of his freshman year gives a pretty accurate picture. In 2002–2003, the Quebec Major Junior Hockey League saw 170,509 patrons rush through its turnstiles. The following year, as the Crosby Caravan trekked across Quebec and the Maritime Provinces, 43,023 more spectators bought tickets. It was a new record for the Q, besting that of the 1999–2000 season. "It was unbelievable," notes Sylvain Couturier, a former L.A. King. "Teams that had been struggling to sell tickets were suddenly seeing standing room only crowds…. It was really something to see how he was bringing fans back to the rinks."

In addition to being a hit with fans, Sidney Crosby, and by extension the league itself, became the focus of intense scrutiny by national and international media alike. The QMJHL, long since a hit with Quebec-based television and radio outlets,

REGULAR SEASON STATS

TEAM	GP	G	A	P	PIM	+/–
2003–2004 Rimouski	59	54	81	135	74	49
2004–2005 Rimouski	62	66	102	168	84	78

PLAYOFF STATS

TEAM	GP	G	A	P	PIM	+/–
2003–2004 Rimouski	9	7	9	16	13	5
2004–2005 Rimouski	13	14	17	31	16	11
Memorial Cup Rimouski	5	6	5	11	6	7

THERE ARE NO TICKETS AVAILABLE FOR TONIGHTS GAME JANUARY 18, 2004

A sign of the times. Sidney Crosby and the Rimouski Oceanic sell out the Molson Coliseum during a January 2004 road trip to the Hub City.

began to attract much attention from networks outside the provincial boundaries.

The thirst that sports television networks and print media had for anything Crosby seemingly could not be quenched. Half-hour television sports magazines were beginning "Crosby Watch" segments, and the previous night's efforts by number 87 and his Rimouski Oceanic teammates were often the leading story in morning sports recaps. Box-score summaries in national daily newspapers throughout the nation detailed the Oceanic's every move.

Whether it be through radio or television or the exploding number of Web sites dedicated to teams or players associated with the Quebec Major Junior Hockey League, the Q had suddenly become extremely hip. For the first time, the QMJHL had become larger than either of its CHL brethren. Considering the struggles of the league only a generation before, the Q's comeback, thanks in large part to Sidney Crosby, was truly grand.

Last but certainly not least, Sidney Crosby's influence on league expansion, as subtle as it might have been, was substantial. Just before Christmas 2004, the QMJHL announced the awarding of

team suffer a bizarre and heart-wrenching 4–3 championship-game loss to Team USA.

Crosby's rookie performance in Helsinki had been a far cry from Ovechkin's World Junior Championship debut in Halifax in 2003. As a seventeen-year-old centreman from Moscow Dynamo, Ovechkin was among the tournament leaders in scoring, and he played an integral role in his country's gold medal victory.

It can often be true that some of our greatest accomplishments are born out of profound disappointment. As much as the 2004 World Junior Championship must have hurt Sidney Crosby, it may have ultimately provided the inspiration and motivation for his greatest moment in the sport. From the time he returned from Europe, his game was simply superb. Despite already owning NHL-calibre skills, the Rimouski star seemed intent on getting even better at every facet of the game.

Canada. The 2004 World Junior Championship would provide him his first genuine opportunity to show the hockey establishment that he belonged in the same company as Alexander Ovechkin, the Russian star who had taken a "leave" from the Russian Elite League to showcase his tremendous skills to the world. Even at sixteen, the talented Crosby seemed primed to challenge Ovechkin's domination of the junior game.

However, as the tournament progressed, it became clear that Sidney Crosby was not yet ready for prime time. Relegated to playing a supporting role, Sidney Crosby failed to put up big numbers. In four round-robin games in which Canada scored an impressive total of 25 goals, Crosby could muster only 3 points. In the semifinal and final games against the Czech Republic and the United States respectively, Crosby contributed only a couple of assists and watched his

In addition to his superlative natural skills, Crosby seemed determined to bring his natural leadership abilities to the forefront. Former Team Canada coach Mario Durocher had an opportunity to see those skills first-hand: "Sidney's teammates instinctively follow his lead," says Durocher. "Sidney leads by example and in the dressing room, and I think that in 2005 he

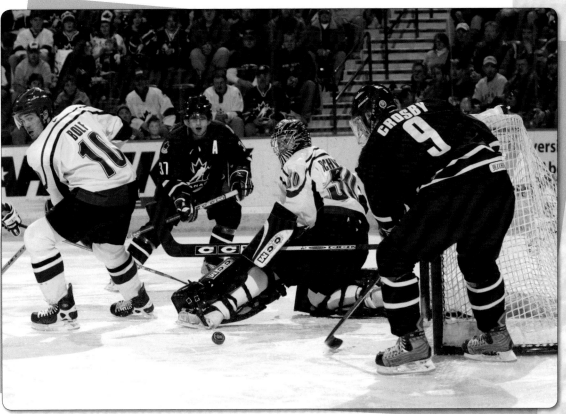

Sidney Crosby gets set to tap in a perfect feed from linemate Patrice Bergeron. Canada defeated the Czech Republic 3–1 to advance to the finals against Russia in the 2005 World Junior Hockey Championship.

wanted to highlight that role." Sidney Crosby seemed comfortable in his role as a calming influence in the dressing room, and as the initial selection camp for the 2005 World Junior Championship grew near, his game was at or near its peak.

At the national team's evaluation camp in July 2005, Team Canada brass instantly recognized the key role the Cole Harbour native would need to play. As a sixteen-year-old, Crosby had come to the final selection camp perhaps willing to take a secondary role in order to make the cut. In 2005, as a returning national team veteran fresh off a spectacular junior season—one that

included winning the CHL's top player award— Crosby would be given a starring role and a spot on the top line.

Throughout the 2005 pre-tournament and round-robin schedule, Crosby's performance was nothing less than spectacular. Having completely put to rest his struggles in Helsinki, Crosby went to work in Grand Forks, racking up eight points on the strength of six goals and two assists. He had put Team Canada on his shoulders and was determined to help carry it into the medal round.

Team Canada defenders team up to stop a Czech Republic
forward from advancing into the Team Canada zone.

Of course, the round-robin portion of the tournament meant relatively little to Team Canada. Since the moment the schedule had been released, the only date on the calendar that held any meaning was January 4, 2005—the championship final. Somehow Crosby must have known deep down that on that date, he and Ovechkin would tangle for the very last time in their amateur careers, with more than just the championship of the world on the line.

2005 World Junior Final
January 4, 2005, Grand Forks, North Dakota

For Sidney Crosby, the night was not about scoring goals and racking up points. No one had ever questioned his ability to put points on the board. It was understood by most that this world junior final was about leadership and the ability to carry a team to a championship. Team Canada would need to put together a sixty-minute effort. Each period of the game would present new and different challenges, and each period saw Sidney Crosby appear to take on a different yet equally important role.

In the first twenty minutes, Crosby played the role of the intimidator. Team Russia, rightfully concerned about the Crosby line's ability to break open a game, was consumed with stopping him and his linemates (Bergeron and Perry), so much so that other Team Canada forward units seemed to be able to penetrate Russia's zone at will. While Russia used its best defensive forwards to try and contain the Crosby trio, talented Team Canada skaters such as Mike Richards, Ryan Getzlaf, and Danny Syvret consistently broke through to create scoring opportunities.

In the second frame, Crosby's killer instinct came to the fore as he helped set up the scoring play that for all intents and purposes put away the Russians. Crosby, who had been dangerous the entire game but had not yet registered a point, connected with Perry and finally Bergeron on a marvellous three-way

ABOVE: A disappointed Sidney Crosby watches Team USA celebrate their gold medal victory over Canada in the 2004 World Junior Hockey Championship.

passing play to give Team Canada an insurmountable 5–1 lead.

In the final period, Crosby's 2004 world junior experience was put to use as he helped calm and reassure his anxious teammates. It is important to remember that in recent years, Team Canada had become notorious for finding ways to lose. In Halifax in 2003, the home team came into the third period with the game under control and a 2–1 lead, only to have Ovechkin and Team Russia wrestle the lead away en route to a 3–2 gold medal victory.

In 2004, in perhaps the most disappointing game in our nation's junior hockey history, Team Canada enjoyed a 3–1 lead entering the third period of the gold medal match. Head coach Mario Durocher had his team playing superbly, and the overwhelmed Americans seemed to be going through the motions when suddenly the momentum swung inexplicably. Team Canada gave up three unanswered goals in the final twenty minutes to allow Team USA to steal the gold medal with a 4–3 come-from-behind win.

In 2005, Sidney Crosby and his mates were not about to let that happen.

In the final period in Grand Forks, Crosby could be seen talking constantly to teammates, giving directives and encouragement. Right up until the final siren, Crosby was directing traffic, refusing to allow teammates to lose their focus or celebrate too early. As the final seconds ticked off the clock, junior hockey fans around the world knew they had witnessed something very special. Team Canada had proved they were the best … and Sidney Crosby had surged past the Russian rebel to become hockey's best teenage player.

Anyone using the next day's newspaper box score to get his or her sole take on the game might have seen Crosby's lone assist and presumed he'd had an uneventful evening. Nothing could be further from the truth. Sidney Crosby played a complete sixty minutes; he had been everything coach Brent Sutter had hoped for.

Of course January 4, 2005, was significant for Sidney Crosby not only in terms of his rivalry with Alexander Ovechkin; it also marked the night that Sidney Crosby locked in his status as professional hockey's next icon. "No doubt about it. Sidney Crosby's performance at the championships solidified his status as the NHL's next superstar in waiting," says Shattuck–St. Mary's director of hockey operations, J. P. Parisé.

It had become apparent during the 2005 World Junior Championship that Sidney Crosby's leadership skills had become as much a part of his game as his on-ice skills. After watching him perform in Grand Forks, the suits at NHL headquarters must have realized they had finally found that great young talent who possessed the personal strength, desire, and skill set to become the unquestioned leader of the game.

Since his amazing stint at Shattuck–St. Mary's in 2002–2003, many had hoped that Sidney Crosby could be groomed as Mario Lemieux's heir. On the strength of his performance at the world juniors, Sidney Crosby proved he had the ability to take the lead among NHL superstars as the sport was about to take dead aim once again at the lucrative American and European markets.

FACING PAGE: Sidney Crosby straddles the blue line in a 2003 World Junior game against Switzerland.

BELOW: A Team USA forward moves around Team Canada's Sidney Crosby in the final of the 2004 World Junior Hockey Championship in Helsinki, Finland.

ABOVE TOP: Adam Blanchette of the Moncton Wildcats tries to block Sidney Crosby during an October 31, 2004, match. Crosby scored two goals and an assist in the game, but the Wildcats would eventually prevail by a score of 9–5.

ABOVE BOTTOM: Sidney Crosby attempts to deflect the puck past Moncton Wildcat goaltender Corey Crawford. Crawford and Crosby may soon renew their acquaintance at the NHL level. Crosby, of course, is the first-overall pick of the Penguins while Crawford is a second-round selection of the Chicago Blackhawks.

his first of the tournament to even the match at three.

As the extra session got underway, it was clear that it was just a matter of time before the Knights would break through. At 9:36 of overtime, Methot ended the best game of his career by depositing a sweet feed from Perry after the winger had successfully pulled keeper Desjardins out of position. "It was unbelievable. Corey made a beautiful pass right across the slot," said the eighteen-year-old Methot. "I saw the goalie cheating over to Corey's side. I just shot it as high as I could on him and it went in" (SLAM! sports).

Sidney Crosby and the Oceanic were stung by the game-one collapse. After a league playoff that saw them barely break a sweat on their way to winning the President's Cup, the loss to the Knights had already placed Crosby and company in a bit of trouble. The QMJHL champ could not afford another loss, and there would be little time to make the required adjustments as the gritty Ottawa 67's hockey club waited in the wings.

Two things must have become obvious to the Oceanic as they prepared to play for their playoff lives: If they were to reach Sunday's final, two very important lessons from their opening-game loss

needed to be acknowledged. First, after blowing a two-goal lead to London, it was obvious to some that their defensive game and their goaltending were not strong enough to protect a lead. Rimouski would therefore need to hold the pedal to the metal on offence and win games by scoring a lot of goals. Second, for the Oceanic to win the rest of their games, a must considering their 4–3 loss to London, Sidney Crosby would need to play an even bigger role in their success than first thought.

From the drop of the puck in their game against Ottawa, it appeared both lessons had been taken to heart. Having been denied on a glorious scoring opportunity just seconds into the contest, Crosby shrewdly

THEY PLAYED KIND OF PHYSICAL AGAINST US BUT WE STILL WORKED HARD TO CRASH THE NET AND TRY TO MAKE THINGS HAPPEN.

used his strength to buy time and space in front of the Ottawa net before one-timing a pass from Oceanic captain Marc-Antoine Pouliot past 67's keeper Danny Battochio at the 11:18 mark.

After the Oceanic and 67's traded goals late in the first period, Sidney Crosby helped Rimouski regain its two-goal lead by engineering one of the prettiest plays in the tournament. In the opening minute of play in the second, Crosby, defenceman Patrick Coulombe, and Pouliot combined on a slick three-way passing play, with Pouliot depositing Coulombe's feed into the back of the Ottawa net.

The 67's would ultimately come back and make a game of it, but Dany Roussin's goal at the

7:00 mark of the third proved to be the game winner, securing the Oceanic's first win and a spot in Friday's tiebreaker. "We just tried to move the puck and use our speed—that's what we have to do," said Crosby, who tied Corey Perry of the London Knights for the tournament scoring lead with four points in two games. "They played kind of physical against us but we still worked hard to crash the net and try to make things happen" (SLAM! sports).

The win against Ottawa was the perfect cap on a day that saw Crosby rewarded with the CHL's top honour. The Rimouski Oceanic star took home the league's top individual award—the Reebok CHL Player of the Year. Crosby, who led the CHL with 66 goals and 168 points in sixty-two regular season games, became the first player in CHL history to win the trophy twice. He was also player of the year as a sixteen-year-old in 2004. "It's special for sure," Crosby said. "I just came into the season wanting to improve but at the same time I didn't want to put pressure on myself to win it again. For sure it's special to win it two years in a row" (SLAM! sports). Crosby also took home the CGC Sheetrock Top Scorer award and the Canada Post Cup three-stars award.

As special and as eventful as the day was for Crosby and his teammates, once again there would be little time to enjoy the moment. Rimouski was right back on the ice the next day in a critical match that would see the Oceanic attempt to eliminate the defending champion Kelowna Rockets.

The situation for Kelowna was dire. Round-robin losses to Ottawa and London meant the Rockets could not afford a defeat at the hands of the QMJHL entry. For Rimouski, a victory would send them directly into Saturday's semifinal match and earn them a valuable day off on Friday.

Determined to avoid a scenario that would see them play three games in three days, the Oceanic finally got some welcome offensive contribution from their second line. Zbynek Hrdel, who had been stealthily quiet during the first two games, opened the scoring for Rimouski late in the first period. Hrdel picked up a rebound from a Mario Scalzo Jr. knuckleball and slipped it behind Rocket goaltender Kristofer Westblom.

The match against Kelowna was never really in doubt. Following Hrdel's icebreaker, the Oceanic got goals from Crosby, Scalzo, and François Bolduc to open up a healthy 4–1 lead. Blake Comeau's deuce in the third period put a bit of a scare into the Oceanic, but ultimately the double blue would hang on and take the contest 4–3.

For the first time in the tournament, Rimouski played a complete team game. The Oceanic turned in a terrific game from top to bottom against the WHL champion, getting contributions from every forward and defensive unit as well as top-notch goaltending from a determined Desjardins.

Quick FACTS

Fellow Shattuck–St. Mary's grad and good friend Jack Johnson was also selected in the first round of the 2005 NHL entry draft. Johnson, selected third overall by the Carolina Hurricanes, is expected to be a Norris Trophy candidate of the future.

Sidney Crosby plants himself in front of Halifax Moosehead goalkeeper Jason Churchill during game four of the 2005 league finals at the Metro Centre. Crosby and company would sweep the much-anticipated final series in four games.

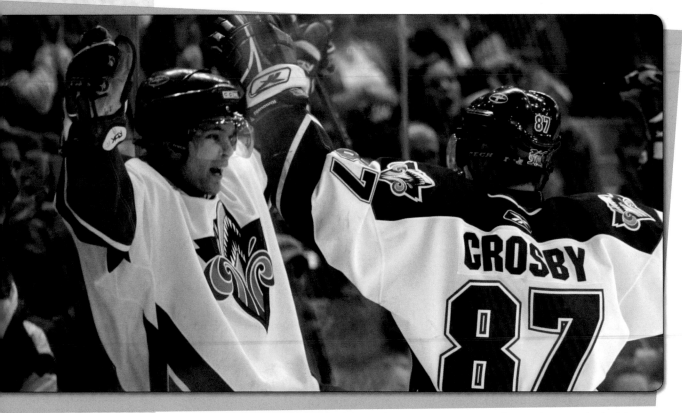

As was the case in games one and two, Sidney Crosby posted a goal and assist and was terrific at both ends of the ice. For the second time in three games, Crosby was awarded a game-star selection.

With their portion of the round-robin tournament finished, the Rimouski Oceanic had more than forty-eight hours to plan and prepare for their semifinal rematch against the Ottawa 67's. Although still somewhat disappointed that their players had let the opening-round match against London slip through their fingers, the Oceanic brass had to be pleased with the way their team had rebounded, and extremely happy with the performance of their top star.

However, as well as Sidney Crosby had been playing, he had not shown his A game yet. Unfortunately for the Ottawa 67's, Sidney Crosby was about to reach that level with a semifinal game for the ages.

In a game dubbed by some "the Crosby Show," the Cole Harbour native scored three goals and two assists to pace the Oceanic to a 7–4 semifinal win. If ever there was a game that underscored Crosby's killer instinct, it was this one. It seemed that every time the Oceanic needed to fend off the 1999 national champions, Crosby would mastermind another successful scoring drive.

Moncton's Kevin Glode gets the stick up high on Sidney Crosby during a QMJHL regular season game in 2005.

> *CROSBY'S LINE GOT OFF TO A QUICK START IN THE OPENING PERIOD OF GAME 1, AND LONDON KNEW THEY COULD NOT EXPECT TO COME BACK FROM A TWO GOAL DEFICIT AGAIN.*
>
> —Brad Crossley, head coach of the Dartmouth Subways

Quick FACTS

Sidney Crosby will attempt to help keep the Penguins' perfect Stanley Cup–final record intact. The Pittsburgh club is batting .1000 in Stanley Cup–final play, having won their only two appearances in 1991 and 1992.

Crosby opened the scoring for Rimouski less than two minutes into the game and appeared to be a threat to score each and every time he picked up the puck. Whether it be on special teams or five on five, in the offensive or defensive zone, taking faceoffs or playing the wing, Crosby was absolutely dominating.

Number 87 would score a goal in each of the regulation periods, including a floater from centre ice that caught nothing but mesh. The hat trick, in addition to assists on goals by Pouliot and Scalzo, secured Crosby's third game-star selection in four games.

Crosby's play in the semifinal win over Ottawa left many shaking their heads over just how good number 87 was. Just when you thought you had seen the kid do it all, he would come up with a performance like he did in the Memorial Cup and raise the bar even higher. In true Crosby style, however, he was not about to take sole credit for the performance. "We play as a team, we win as a team, we lose as a team," is an earlier Crosby quote that refkects the young man's thoughts following the post-game ceremonies (Crosby Connection).

The Rimouski Oceanic were peaking at just the right time. As difficult as it would be to beat a rested London Knights team the following afternoon, Crosby's performance in the semifinal must have put London on notice that Sidney Crosby was coming into the final firing on all cylinders.

And Then There Were Two

Before the final game, the Knights' coaching staff recognized the importance of denying Rimouski's top line of Crosby, Pouliot, and Roussin. "Crosby's line got off to a quick start in the opening period of game one," notes Brad Crossley, head coach of the Dartmouth Subways, "and London knew they could not expect to come back from a two-goal deficit again." Dale Hunter, seemingly acknowledging the fact that defenceman Daniel Girardi failed to control Crosby in the opener, once again handed the job of neutralizing the tournament's top scorer to power forward Brandon Prust. It was this matchup that very likely would determine the 2005 national junior championship.

The John Labatt Centre was electric as the starting players skated to centre ice for the puck drop. For hockey purists, the rumble between London and Rimouski, two teams that had equal amounts of respect and dislike for each other, was perfect. The number one and two ranked teams in the nation were finally settling the issue … *mano-a-mano.*

In hindsight, the Oceanic probably wished they had handled the opening five-minute stanza better. Eric Neilson and Jean-Sébastien Côté, perhaps too concerned with establishing an early physical presence, picked up consecutive cross-checking infractions to put the Oceanic two men down. Dan Fritsche, the London Knights veteran, continued his strong tournament play as he beat Cedrik Desjardins to open the scoring four minutes into the match.

Unlike previous tournament matches, Sidney Crosby did not get off to a fast start. For the second consecutive meeting, Prust, the six-foot native of London, was doing an effective job of negating the Oceanic superstar. With Crosby struggling to find skating room, the Oceanic's offensive game ground to a standstill, and the Knights began to assert control over the championship game.

Whether it was the fatigue factor (two sudden-death games in less than twenty-four hours) or a case of nerves setting in, the Rimouski Oceanic looked nothing like the well-oiled machine that had steamrolled over Ottawa in the semifinal. By the end of the second period, markers by Bryan Rodney and David Bolland had given the Knights a seemingly insurmountable 3–0 lead.

Despite Doris Labonte's attempts to spring free his superstar, the Oceanic simply did not seem up to the task. The Knights defence,

Sidney Crosby eyes the net as he prepares to blast another powerful shot at an opposing goalie.

London's Trevor Kell finds himself in a one-on-one battle with Rimouski's Sidney Crosby during the opening match of the 2005 Memorial Cup. The OHL champion would eventualy subdue the Oceanic 4–3 in the extra-session thriller on a goal by defenceman Marc Methot.

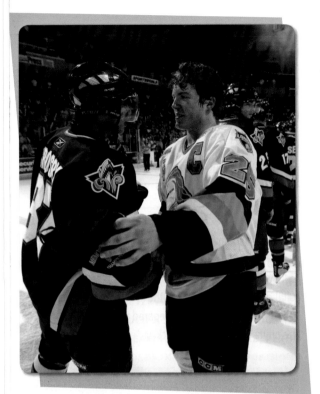

which had been seen by some as the team's Achilles heel, had thrown a suffocating blanket over the Oceanic attack. If Rimouski fans had hoped the intermission would help turn the tide, Edmonton Oilers prospect Robbie Schremp quickly put an end to those hopes.

With a final game performance that may have sold Oiler GM Kevin Lowe on his NHL credentials, the Fulton, New York, native Shcremp snapped a wrist shot past Desjardins early in the third, signalling the end of the night for Desjardins.

As the seconds wound down on the season, it was apparent that the London Knights had bluntly ended the debate as to which team was Canada's

best. London's 4–0 shutout of Rimouski was dominant from start to finish, leaving no doubt that the 2004–2005 edition of the London Knights would go down as one of the truly great teams in CHL history. For the Knights and their fans, their fortieth year in operation would be one not soon forgotten. For starters, London had reeled off a CHL-record thirty-one-game undefeated streak that broke a decades-old mark set by the Brandon Wheat Kings. The 2004–2005 Knights also became the first team in OHL history to record back-to-back fifty-win and 100-point seasons. Most important of all, the London Knights had put an end to a near half-century of drought, bringing home their first-ever national junior title.

For Sidney Crosby, it must have been a devastating loss, perhaps in some respects comparable to the gold medal game defeat at the hands of the Americans in January of 2004. Brandon Prust had done an exemplary job of shadowing Sidney Crosby, perhaps even providing him with an invaluable lesson.

Sidney Crosby is an incredible talent, very aware that in every game he plays as a pro, there will be a Brandon Prust waiting to try and shut him down. Whether it be Kris Draper (Red Wings), Mike Peca (Oilers), Jere Lehtinen (Stars), or John Madden (Devils), over the course of his career, number 87 will be

London Knight captain Danny Syvret, number 25, and Sidney Crosby, number 87, exchange best wishes following the Knights' Memorial Cup clinching win. Syvret and Crosby were both part of the national junior team that won gold in Grand Forks, North Dakota, in January of 2005.

Quick FACTS

Sidney Crosby will be trying to lead Pittsburgh back to the Stanley Cup finals for the first time in fourteen years. In 1992 Lemieux, Jaromir Jagr, and Ron Francis carried the Pens to a four-game sweep of the Chicago Blackhawks.

It may not have the history of a Madison Square Garden or a Montreal Forum, but the Mellon Arena in Pittsburgh will host many sellout crowds in 2005–2006 as the Penguins faithful flock to see Sidney Crosby in the beloved black and gold.

Also, the National Hockey League is removing the centre red line for the 2005–2006 season. This long overdue move is also going to increase Sidney Crosby's point total because it will accentuate his ability to pass the puck. For those lucky enough to see him play on a nightly basis in the Q, it is amazing just how good he is at putting the puck right on the tape of his teammates' sticks as they are breaking full stride in the neutral zone. With the disappearance of the red line this year at the professional level, Crosby is going to have a field day launching big bombs from inside his own blue line.

In the past, the centre red line took away the speed game and limited forwards' ability to use their skating skills to put pressure on defenders. One can only imagine how many more points Gretzky might have accumulated had the red line not hindered his ability to hit a streaking Jari Kurri or Mark Messier. Fortunately for Crosby, it's an impediment he will not have to endure, and its worth in terms of adding to his numbers will be priceless.

Finally, a couple of NHL decisions affecting the goalies should also add a slew of points to Crosby's total. In the past, some goaltenders bla-tantly disregarded the rules governing the size of their equipment. (Anyone who remembers former Flyers goaltender Garth Snow's attire is familiar with the problem.) The days when goaltenders could simply stop opposing forwards by getting bigger are over. This rule could pump the new NHL full of offensive production. With more net attracting Sidney Crosby's pinpoint blasts, don't be surprised to see the kid hit the 50-goal mark before he finishes his third year on the circuit.

Plus, with goaltenders such as New Jersey's Martin Brodeur and Montreal's José Théodore now limited in their ability to clear the puck out of trouble, forwards who can forecheck will flourish. Number 87 has been the single best forechecker in the CHL since he arrived in Rimouski in the fall of 2003. With Crosby's great skating ability and forechecking prowess forcing defenders into coughing up the puck on a regular basis, and with the new rules limiting the goalies' ability to relieve that pressure by chasing down the puck and dumping it out of the zone, Sidney Crosby is going to have a marked increase in scoring opportunities—and you can bet he is going to cash in on most of them.

Hitting 3,000 points may be Sidney Crosby's biggest hurdle in reaching hockey superstardom; winning the Stanley Cup may come a little more easily. The signing of a historic collective bargaining agreement (CBA) earlier this year, coupled with Pittsburgh's burgeoning young talent base, will increase Crosby's chances of accumulating a few Stanley Cup rings as a member of the Penguins.

The 2005–2006 Pittsburgh Penguins are a mix of proven veterans and exciting new prospects. In this picture Mark Recchi, a talented free agent from the Flyers, sits with the Pens' number-one pick.

Being shadowed by some of the best checkers in the NHL will be something Sidney Crosby will have to get used to game in and game out. In this opening night bout in New Jersey, Jay Pandolfo of the Devils is given the task of shadowing the league's top pick.

The collective bargaining agreement, which features a salary cap of approximately $39 million across the board, was signed in July of 2005 by representatives of the NHL and the players' association. Although the document is seen as a positive step forward by all NHL clubs, it is especially welcomed by teams like the Pittsburgh Penguins, which can now realistically hope to have economic parity with big-market clubs, along with a chance to sign that young talent that will help them compete for the Stanley Cup on a yearly basis.

The new agreement is already allowing Penguins management to go out and sign key free agents who in the past might have been too pricey. More important, it will allow general manager

Craig Patrick to sign and keep the good young talent it has now…and there is plenty of it!

Sidney Crosby is the best player on what is a young and extremely talented hockey club. "The Pittsburgh Penguins, thanks to the astute judgement of GM Patrick and his scouting department, have drafted exceptionally well in the past few years," says Acadie-Bathurst Titan general manager Sylvain Couturier. The club is virtually stacked with all-star talent at every position.

In net, arguably the most important position in the game, the Penguins have the hottest goaltending prospect to come along in almost a decade. After a stellar season in the AHL with the Wilkes-Barre/Scranton Penguins, former

Cape Breton Screaming Eagle Marc-André Fleury is prepared to step up to the big time and become the main cog in the Penguins' drive back to the Stanley Cup. In addition to Fleury, the Pens own the rights to hulking defenceman Brooks Orpik, slick playmaking forward Ryan Malone, and perhaps the most naturally talented young hockey player ever to come out of Europe, Evgeni Malkin of Russia. And then of course…there is Sidney Crosby.

There isn't a superlative around that has not been used to describe his game. Sidney Crosby's skating is better than most anyone presently in the NHL, and his passing ability is finally getting the recognition it deserves. His shot is already one of the hardest and most accurate in the NHL. He can take important faceoffs, and he is such a smart player that coaches want him out on the ice in the last minute of important games. Sidney Crosby hits, Sidney Crosby scores, Sidney Crosby leads…and with this talented group of young Penguins, it may be his leadership abilities that become his largest contribution.

The new-look National Hockey League will be the perfect stage for Crosby to show his stuff. If the NHL continues to find new ways to allow him and the bumper crop of young talent to flourish and make the game everything it can be, then the dream of making hockey a legitimate top-four sport in North America will come true.

In addition to rule changes, Sidney Crosby's short-term impact has centred around providing the NHL with something it has not had in a decade…optimism. After suffering through a prolonged stretch where the NHL was virtually forgotten, Sidney Crosby has once again made professional hockey a going concern.

The media, especially American media, which had ignored the NHL in recent times, have suddenly embraced the sport once again. Large American news organizations, known for covering only negative hockey stories such as the Todd Bertuzzi suspension, have begun to run stories on the revival of professional hockey and the young phenom responsible for its rise from the ashes. Even Jay Leno, an ardent hockey fan, has gotten into the act by welcoming Crosby to the *Tonight Show* on August 4, 2005. The last time the NHL felt this good about itself, Mark Messier and the New York Rangers were carrying Lord Stanley's Cup around Madison Square Garden, with the Garden faithful cheering their approval in unison.

One need only look at the buzz that has surrounded the league since the 2005 lottery and entry draft. American networks, which had seemingly sworn off ever covering NHL news again, have suddenly bought in on the excitement, covering the draft in a way they have not in over a decade. Whether online, through cable or mainstream television news outlets, or through

Quick FACTS

The NHL came perilously close to losing Sidney Crosby's services for the 2005–2006 season. Having lost an entire season (2004–2005) to a lockout, the league and the players' association had to burn the midnight oil in order to successfully iron out a collective bargaining agreement for the 2005–2006 season.

In a fitting farewell to his Quebec Major Junior Hockey League career, Sidney Crosby's Rimouski Oceanic swept his hometown Halifax Mooseheads in four games to win the 2005 league championship.

Quick FACTS

Sidney Crosby came very close to calling Hollywood home. At the NHL draft lottery in July 2005, the Disney-owned Anaheim Mighty Ducks came within a whisker of winning the Sidney Crosby sweepstakes.

Sidney Crosby put up outstanding numbers in his two years in Rimouski. In 2003–2004, Sidney's first year in the province of Quebec, he led the QMJHL in scoring with 54 goals and 81 assist for 135 points. He followed up in 2004–2005 with another productive season, scoring an amazing 168 points in sixty-two games.

sports radio, the arrival of number 87 has captured the attention of millions. Entire blogs are now dedicated to the young man from Cole Harbour.

Interest in NHL clothing and memorabilia, especially those carrying the Penguins logo, is once again finding a mass market. Season ticket sales, which have sometimes been a concern in the past, appear to be finding buyers in every market. The pre-CBA concern that fans would punish the teams by staying away in droves does not seem to be the case early on. Anyone connected to the league would readily admit that Sidney Crosby is one of the major reasons all these good things are happening.

One of the amazing things about professional hockey is that once in a generation it places before us an athlete who actually reminds us why we love the sport so much. Sidney Crosby is special in the eyes of Canadians because he has the ability to make us recall what it is about the game of hockey that we cherish.

Sidney Crosby is about speed and power, fire and finesse. His game is about creativity and skill, but it can also be about the survival of the fittest and playing by the rules of the jungle. When you watch Sidney Crosby, you are watching the

game of hockey as it was meant to be played, and the anticipation of seeing the game played in such a manner has fans excited about what it means for their favourite sport.

Sidney Crosby has played only a handful of exhibition and regular season games. The Pittsburgh Penguins' first-overall pick has not even begun to scratch the surface of what will undoubtedly be an incredible professional hockey career, but already the similarities between Crosby and another legendary athlete are unmistakable.

In 1984, a struggling National Basketball Association welcomed a North Carolina Tar Heel by the name of Michael Jordan into the league. Years prior to his arrival, the NBA was a second-division professional sports league struggling to fill its buildings and desperate to find a way into the hearts and minds of basketball fans across North America. From the moment Air Jordan played his first game as a Chicago Bull until he retired from the game in 2003, he was the cornerstone of his sport, and his popularity was the driving force behind the NBA's emergence as a top-four professional sports league with a worldwide popularity that now rivals the sport of soccer.

To some, asking Sidney Crosby to do for the NHL what Jordan did for the NBA is asking too much…but Sidney Crosby's record of taking the teams and leagues he plays for to greater heights is impeccable. In the early part of this decade, Sidney Crosby helped take the Dartmouth Subway AAA midget club and make it one of the most noteworthy in the nation; a year later, number 87 took a successful prep-school program at

The mentor and the student. Sidney Crosby will have the added benefit of playing and living with the legendary Mario Lemieux in his inaugural season in the NHL.

Quick
FACTS

In dominating fashion, Sidney Crosby and Team Canada methodically disposed of hockey powers the Czech Republic and Russia in the medal round of the 2005 World Junior Championship. The 6–1 title-game victory over Team Russia gave Canada its eleventh world junior gold medal.

In the 2005 World Junior Championship in Grand Forks, Sidney Crosby played on perhaps the best junior hockey line ever assembled. Crosby's linemates for the tournament were Boston Bruins' budding star Patrice Bergeron and London Knights standout Corey Perry.

Shattuck–St. Mary's and made it one of the more recognizable hockey programs in the continent. In 2003, Sidney Crosby helped take a Rimouski Oceanic franchise that was mired in last place to within one game of a Memorial Cup national championship, making the QMJHL the most talked about league in junior hockey in the process.

As with many things, it will be the journey rather than the destination that is truly important. In a decade's time, we will be able to look back with more certainty and see exactly where Sidney Crosby ranks among the all-time greats of the game, but in the meantime, know that you are watching a remarkably talented player who is about to make all of us proud.

ABOVE: The curtain is about to open on another NHL season as parents Troy and Trina Crosby and agent Pat Brisson watch Sidney prepare for his first-ever regular season game against the Devils.

Top

MOST MEMORABLE GAMES

Game 10

WHEN: April 24, 2002

WHERE: Bathurst, New Brunswick

TEAMS: Dartmouth Subway AAA versus Red Deer Chiefs

This game catapulted Sidney Crosby into the national hockey limelight.

In a round-robin game at the national midget championship, held at the K. C. Irving Regional Centre, Sidney Crosby scored three goals and added two assists in the first period of a game against the midget powerhouse Red Deer Chiefs.

Sidney Crosby and his Dartmouth Subway AAA club eventually lost to the Chiefs 8–6, but Crosby's performance was recognized nationally as a breakthrough effort that solidified his status as the nation's top midget prospect.

Game 9

WHEN: April 6, 2003

WHERE: Laurel, Maryland

TEAMS: Shattuck–St. Mary's Sabres versus Team Illinois

Memorable game number nine occurred in the spring of 2003 when Sidney Crosby led the Shattuck–St. Mary's Sabres to a national championship win over Team Illinois.

For Sidney Crosby, the season-ending victory over Illinois capped an unbelievable year of hockey in which the rookie scored 72 goals in only fifty-seven games. The 2002–2003 season may have been the most significant in his career because it marked the beginning of his ascent to hockey stardom.

"Sidney Crosby's year at Shattuck–St. Mary's was a definitive one for the young man. It was the year that everyone began to sit up and take notice," says Shattuck–St. Mary's director of hockey, J. P. Parisé. "Suddenly Sidney Crosby had become more than just a good hockey player. He had become a star, and the whispers about this kid's potential greatness began to grow louder."

Game 8

WHEN: November 28, 2003

WHERE: Rimouski, Quebec

TEAMS: Rimouski Oceanic versus Quebec Remparts

This game was certainly memorable for Sidney Crosby, but for all the wrong reasons.

Early in his rookie season in Rimouski, Sidney Crosby scored a spectacular goal using a lacrosse-style move. The Oceanic forward picked the puck up from the ice with the blade of his stick and shovelled a waist-high flick past a stunned Quebec keeper.

In a lot of hockey circles, the goal smacked of showboating and disrespect for an opponent who was already getting beaten badly. The most stinging criticism of Crosby's feat came from CBC broadcaster Don Cherry. Cherry, host of the popular *Hockey Night in Canada* segment Coach's Corner, called Crosby to the carpet for what he thought was a blatant attempt to show up his opponent.

In time the controversy died down, and Sidney Crosby, perhaps learning a valuable lesson in on-ice etiquette, never again used the amazing move made fashionable by University of Michigan forward Mike Legg back in the late 1990s.

Game 7

WHEN: October 16, 2003

WHERE: Halifax, Nova Scotia

TEAMS: Rimouski Oceanic versus Halifax Mooseheads

Sidney Crosby's first game at the Halifax Metro Centre as a member of the Rimouski Oceanic was truly dramatic. In recent times, the Metro Centre had been home to many special sporting events, but few could match the excitement and anticipation of Crosby's QMJHL homecoming.

Sidney Crosby's assist on a Danny Stewart goal with forty-three seconds left in the final frame gave the Oceanic an exciting 2–1 victory in front of a capacity crowd of more than 10,000.

This game would mark the beginning of an intense and sometimes nasty rivalry between the two squads. Ultimately, Sidney Crosby and Rimouski would win out in the biggest match between the two sides when his team swept the Mooseheads in the 2004–2005 QMJHL finals.

Game 6

WHEN: December 28, 2003

WHERE: Helsinki, Finland

TEAMS: Team Canada versus Team Switzerland

Sidney Crosby's goal in the last minute of the game, a neat deposit off a pass from teammate Dion Phaneuf, broke one of the more cherished records at the World Junior Championship.

At sixteen years, four months, and twenty-four days, Crosby became the youngest player ever to score at the championship. The puck is now on display at the Hockey Hall of Fame in Toronto.

Sidney Crosby would go on to score five points in his world junior hockey debut and take home a silver medal after Team Canada lost the title match to Team USA 4–3.

Game 5

WHEN: April 23, 2005

WHERE: Chicoutimi, Quebec

TEAMS: Rimouski Oceanic versus Chicoutimi Sagueneens

On April 23, 2005, in a Quebec Major Junior Hockey League playoff game against the Chicoutimi Sagueneens, Sidney Crosby scored six points in one of the most dominating one-game performances in league playoff history.

Crosby's goal and five assists led the way in his team's 11–1 white-wash of their semifinal opponent. The Oceanic would take the series in five games and go on to defeat Halifax in the league final.

"That was the best game I ever saw Sidney play," says long-time Oceanic fan J. C. Duclos. "It seemed like every time he touched the puck, Rimouski went up the ice and scored."

Game

WHEN: January 30, 2004

WHERE: Chicoutimi, Quebec

TEAMS: Rimouski Oceanic versus Chicoutimi Sagueneens

In this regular season game against the Sagueneens, Sidney Crosby scored his forty-third goal of the season, breaking the rookie goal-scoring total of Tampa Bay Lightning star Vincent Lecavalier.

Sidney Crosby would go on to score an amazing 54 goals for the Oceanic in 2003–2004, establishing a number of scoring marks that may never be equalled.

Game

WHEN: September 12, 2003

WHERE: Rouyn-Noranda, Quebec

TEAMS: Rimouski Oceanic versus Rouyn-Noranda Huskies

On September 12, 2003, Sidney Crosby began his QMJHL career with a game against the Rouyn-Noranda Huskies.

The Dave Keon Arena, filled with national and international media, Quebec Major Junior Hockey League VIPs, and boisterous and energetic Huskies fans, had never quite witnessed an opening night like this.

In true Crosby fashion, number 87 displayed his flare for the dramatic as he scored a third period hat trick to help his team come from behind and defeat the Huskies 4–3.

Game 2

WHEN: May 28, 2005

WHERE: London, Ontario

TEAMS: Rimouski Oceanic versus Ottawa 67's

Sidney Crosby's performance in the semifinal of the Memorial Cup will go down as one of the finest … if not the finest. The Oceanic power forward scored five points and was a tower of strength at both ends of the ice.

Number 87 scored three goals and added two assists in addition to winning a number of key faceoffs in Rimouski's 7–4 win over the Ottawa 67's. The win put the Oceanic into the following afternoon's Memorial Cup final against the host London Knights.

Crosby's approach to the semifinal? "We just tried to move the puck and use our speed, that's what we have to do," said the game's first star. Crosby would later add, "They played kind of physical against us but we still worked hard to crash the net and try to make things happen" (SLAM! sports).

Game 1

WHEN: January 4, 2005

WHERE: Grand Forks, North Dakota

TEAMS: Team Canada versus Team Russia

On January 4, 2005, Sidney Crosby led Team Canada to its first World Junior Championship gold medal since 1997. Crosby and his Team Canada mates proved they should go down as the best team ever as they thoroughly defeated Russia 6–1.

Crosby recorded only one point in the victory but was a dominant force throughout the game. The big challenge with Alexander Ovechkin never materialized as he was out by the second period with a shoulder injury. "This is a dream come true. I am just happy to have gotten the opportunity to play with these guys. We know how hard this is. Everything we have done for the past three weeks has paid off," said Crosby (SLAM! sports), who finished the tournament with nine points.

Coaches' Forum

Q&A: ABOUT CROSBY, THE NHL, AND THE GAME OF HOCKEY

ON SEPTEMBER 21, 2005, SIDNEY CROSBY BEGAN HIS PROFESSIONAL HOCKEY CAREER WITH A BANG, NOTCHING HIS FIRST POINT WITH AN ASSIST ON MARK RECCHI'S FIRST PERIOD MARKER IN AN EXHIBITION GAME AGAINST THE BOSTON BRUINS. BY ALL ACCOUNTS HIS PLAY IN CAMP AND DURING THE PENGUINS' PRE-SEASON WAS IMPRESSIVE, AND IT CERTAINLY LOOKS AS IF NUMBER 87 IS ABOUT TO MEET THE EXPECTATIONS PLACED BEFORE HIM.

TO DISCUSS THESE EXPECTATIONS AND TO FIELD QUESTIONS ABOUT WHAT THE FUTURE HOLDS FOR SIDNEY CROSBY, THE NATIONAL HOCKEY LEAGUE, AND THE GAME OF HOCKEY IN GENERAL ARE THREE EXCEPTIONAL COACHES:

MARIO DUROCHER was Sidney Crosby's coach for the 2004 World Junior Championship in Helsinki, Finland. Durocher is presently head coach of the Acadie-Bathurst Titan of the QMJHL.

JEAN-PAUL (J. P.) PARISÉ is the director of hockey operations at Shattuck–St. Mary's. Parisé was also a member of the famous Team Canada from the 1972 Summit Series.

BRAD CROSSLEY is the head coach of the Dartmouth Subway AAA midget hockey club.

MARIO DUROCHER, HOW DIFFICULT WAS IT TO SELECT A SIXTEEN-YEAR-OLD SIDNEY CROSBY TO THE NATIONAL TEAM IN 2004?

MARIO DUROCHER: Selecting Sidney to our team in 2004 was not difficult at all. The young man was having a terrific year in Rimouski, and he had a good selection camp as well. Because we had veterans on that team like Danny Paille and Marc-André Fleury who provided the leadership, Sidney was allowed to just play his game and not have to worry about trying to do too much. Sidney certainly earned his way onto the team; it was a great experience for him, and he was that much better for it in 2005.

J. P. PARISÉ, WHAT DO YOU THINK SIDNEY'S GREATEST ASSET IS?

J. P. PARISÉ: I think Sidney's greatest asset both on and off the ice is his intelligence. He has so much natural skill that we often forget about how smart a hockey player he really is. Sidney's composure and smarts are the main reasons you put him out on the ice in the last minute of an important game … because you know he is going to make wise decisions.

J. P. PARISÉ, SIDNEY'S FORMER TEAMMATE AT SHATTUCK–ST. MARY'S AND GOOD BUDDY JACK JOHNSON WAS DRAFTED BY THE NHL'S CAROLINA HURRICANES. WHO WILL WIN THE BATTLE WHEN THEY MEET FOR THE FIRST TIME ON OCTOBER 7?

J. P. PARISÉ: Well, I am pretty sure that Jack will be spending this year in university … but let me tell you, both of these guys are terrific hockey players and will be impact players in the NHL for a long time. Jack is a defenceman of course and Sidney a forward, so comparing the two is difficult … but their first NHL head-to-head battle should be quite something.

HOW LONG WILL IT TAKE SIDNEY CROSBY TO BECOME AN IMPACT PLAYER IN THE NATIONAL HOCKEY LEAGUE?

BRAD CROSSLEY: I think Sidney has already had an impact on the Penguins in terms of getting the fan base excited again. On the ice, of course, it is going to be an adjustment for Sidney, as it is for every rookie in the NHL, but he is such a terrific talent that he is going to make that adjustment quicker than most. And don't forget Sidney Crosby will have a terrific mentor [Mario Lemieux] in Pittsburgh as well.

WHAT HAS BEEN SIDNEY CROSBY'S GREATEST MOMENT IN HOCKEY SO FAR?

MARIO DUROCHER: Personally, I have to go with his gold medal effort at the world championships in 2005. Sidney played so well in Grand Forks, I really think it was his finest hour. I think off the ice you certainly have to include his being selected number one by Pittsburgh … what a great moment that must have been for him.

WHAT DOES SIDNEY CROSBY'S SUCCESS MEAN TO YOUNG HOCKEY PLAYERS IN HALIFAX, AND ALL ACROSS ATLANTIC CANADA?

BRAD CROSSLEY: Sidney is a terrific role model for all young athletes in our region, especially hockey players, and has been for quite some time. Sidney has provided inspiration to a number of young athletes in our region and has proved that if you dedicate yourself to being the best athlete that you can be, there is no reason that with hard work and a little luck you can't get to the top.

MARIO DUROCHER, DO YOU THINK SIDNEY CROSBY WILL BE SELECTED FOR THE TURIN WINTER GAMES OF 2006?

MARIO DUROCHER: Well, certainly if Sidney has a dynamite first half of the regular season, Hockey Canada will give him major consideration. It certainly is very tough, though, considering how deep Canada is at the forward position. Remember that Calgary's Jarome Iginla was not in consideration until the last moment in 2002, and he ended up being a very important member of that gold medal team.

IS SIDNEY CROSBY BIG ENOUGH AND STRONG ENOUGH TO HANDLE THE PHYSICAL PLAY OF THE NHL?

BRAD CROSSLEY: I can tell you first-hand that Sidney Crosby is certainly big enough and strong enough to handle the rough going. Sidney has dominated every division he has ever played in, and a lot of teams have failed in trying to intimidate him. One thing you need to remember, Sidney Crosby is a tough guy, and he never backs away from the physical part of the game.

Quick FACTS

In hockey circles, number 87 is now as famous as Gretzky's number 99 and Mario Lemieux's number 66. Sidney Crosby will not be the only NHLer wearing the number this season, however. Donald Brashear of the Philadelphia Flyers, one of the few players to ever don number 87, will also sport the number that Crosby made famous.

Sidney's first point as a professional hockey player came in a September 21, 2005, exhibition game against the Boston Bruins. He registered an assist on Mark Recchi's first period marker in the Penguins' 5–4 overtime loss.

COACH DUROCHER, WITH ALL OF THE PRESSURE THAT IS GOING TO BE PLACED ON SIDNEY CROSBY'S SHOULDERS, WHAT IS THE BEST PIECE OF ADVICE YOU COULD GIVE HIM AS HE BEGINS HIS ROOKIE SEASON IN THE NHL?

MARIO DUROCHER: I think the best piece of advice I could give to Sidney is just to be himself. Sidney is blessed with all of the skills necessary to succeed. There is no doubt that there are expectations and a lot of pressure, but everywhere he has played he has had that kind of pressure, and he has always lived up to the billing.

MARIO DUROCHER, WHEN YOU WERE COACHING IN LEWISTON, HOW WOULD YOU GUYS TRY TO STOP SIDNEY CROSBY?

MARIO DUROCHER: We were fortunate in Lewiston to play very well against Sidney and the Oceanic … at times it is not as much about trying to stop him as it is trying to not let him beat you by himself. In Lewiston we tried to keep him as far away from the puck as possible. But Sidney is a great player, and he will always make the needed adjustments.

IF YOU COULD USE ONE WORD TO DESCRIBE SIDNEY CROSBY, WHAT WOULD IT BE?

MARIO DUROCHER: Strong.

J. P. PARISÉ: Smart.

BRAD CROSSLEY: Talented.

Paul Arseneault lives in Belledune, New Brunswick, and is a teacher at the middle school level in the Dalhousie/Campbellton/Bathurst district. He has played and coached a number of sports—including hockey—at the minor, senior/intermediate, and college levels, garnering provincial, Maritime, and national championships. Paul has followed Sidney Crosby's career closely since the early 1990s.